THE OFFICIAL **NATIONAL PARK GUIDE**

DARTMOOR

Text by Richard Sale · Photographs by Chris Chapman

SERIES EDITOR **Roly Smith**

PEVENSEY GUIDES

A DAVID & CHARLES BOOK
Copyright © David & Charles
Limited 2000

David & Charles is an F+W Media Inc.
company 4700 East Galbraith Road
Cincinnati, OH 45236

The Pevensey Press is an imprint of
David & Charles

First published in the UK in 2000
Reprinted 2006, 2008, 2011

Map artwork by Chartwell Illustrators

Text copyright © Richard Sale 2000
Photographs copyright © Chris Chapman
2000, except pages 34, 37 & 40 copyright
© Mark Hamblin 2000

ISBN-13: 978-1-8986-3012-8 (paperback)
ISBN-10: 1-8986-3012-7 (paperback)

Book design by
Les Dominey Design Company, Exeter
and printed in China by
Hong Kong Graphics & Printing Limited
for David & Charles
Brunel House   Newton Abbot   Devon

David & Charles publish high quality
books on a wide range of subjects. For
more great book ideas visit:
www.rubooks.co.uk

Contents

Page 1: Medieval cross above Drywell, Widecombe parish
Pages 2–3: Cuckoo Rock with Sheepstor beyond. Cuckoo Rock lies at the head of a valley which is a favourite haunt of the cuckoo
Left: White Lady Waterfall, Lydford Gorge. It is said that if you see a ghostly white lady as you fall down the gorge you will not drown in the river

Front cover: (above) St Michaels at Brent Tor; (below) medieval cross, Week Down; (front flap) dawn from Hound Tor
Back cover: Looking towards Jurston and Shapley Common from Meldon Hill

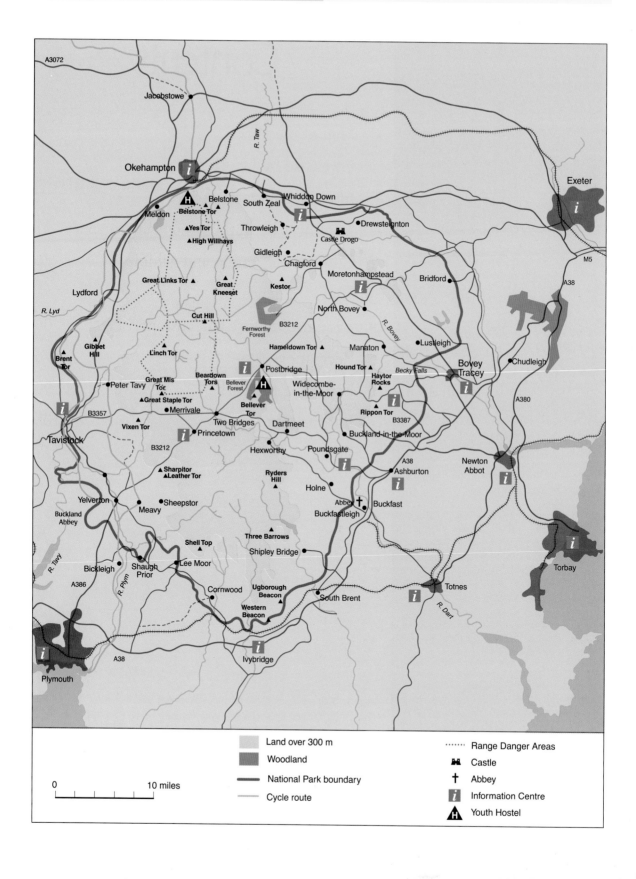

Land over 300 m

Woodland

National Park boundary

Cycle route

Range Danger Areas

Castle

Abbey

Information Centre

Youth Hostel

0   10 miles

Foreword

by Professor Ian Mercer CBE, Secretary General, Association of National Park Authorities

The National Parks of Great Britain are very special places. Their landscapes include the most remote and dramatic hills and coasts in England and Wales, as well as the wild wetlands of the Broads. They still support the farming communities which have fashioned their detail over the centuries. They form the highest rank of the protected areas which society put in place in 1949. So, 1999 saw the fiftieth anniversary of the founding legislation which, incidentally, provided for Areas of Outstanding Natural Beauty, Nature Reserves, Areas of Special Scientific Interest and Long Distance Footpaths, as well as for National Parks.

In the eight years following that, ten Parks were designated. The Lake District, the Peak, Snowdonia and Dartmoor were already well visited, as were the North York Moors, Pembrokeshire Coast, Yorkshire Dales and Exmoor which quickly followed. The Brecon Beacons and Northumberland had their devotees too, though perhaps in lesser numbers then. The special quality of each of these places was already well known, and while those involved may not have predicted the numbers, mobility or aspirations of visitors accurately, the foresight of the landscape protection system cannot be too highly praised.

That system has had to evolve – not just to accommodate visitor numbers, but to meet the pressures flowing from agricultural change, hunger for housing and roadstone, thirst for water, and military manoeuvring – and indeed, the Norfolk and Suffolk Broads were added to the list in 1989. National Parks are now cared for by free-standing authorities who control development, hold land, grant-aid farmers and others, provide wardens, information, car parks and loos, clear footpaths and litter, plant trees and partner many other agents in pursuit of the purposes for which National Parks exist. Those purposes are paramount for all public agencies' consideration when they act within the Parks. They are:

- the conservation of the natural beauty, wildlife and cultural heritage of the area, and
- the promotion of the understanding and enjoyment of its special qualities by the public.

The National Park Authorities must, in pursuing those purposes, foster social and economic well-being. They now bring in some £48 million a year between them to be deployed in the Parks, in addition to normal local public spending.

This book is first a celebration of the National Park, of all its special qualities and of the people whose predecessors produced and maintained the detail of its character. The series to which this book belongs celebrates too the first fifty years of National Park protection in the United Kingdom, the foresight of the founding fathers, and the contributions since of individuals like John Sandford, Reg Hookway and Ron Edwards. The book and the series also mark the work of the present National Park Authorities and their staff, at the beginning of the next fifty years, and of the third millennium of historic time. Their dedication to their Parks is only matched by their aspiration for the sustainable enhancement of the living landscapes for which they are responsible. They need, and hope for, your support.

In the new century, national assets will only be properly maintained if the national will to conserve them is made manifest to national governments. I hope this book will whet your appetite for the National Park, or help you get more from your visit, and provoke you to use your democratic influence on its behalf. In any case it will remind you of the glories of one of the jewels in Britain's landscape crown. Do enjoy it.

Introducing Dartmoor

At the time when reptiles were first colonising the Earth, the land that is now Britain's south-west peninsula – Devon, Cornwall and part of Somerset – was covered by a range of mountains. Into the bases of these mountains molten rock from deep within the Earth was forced. During the aeons of geological time which followed, the mountain tops were eroded by wind and rain, but before the granite – the cooled molten rock – was exposed to the air the south-west was submerged beneath a warm sea.

While dinosaurs roamed the Earth the peninsula remained submerged: not until the giant reptiles had been replaced by mammals was it again pushed above the sea. Now the top surface of rock, a soft chalk formed from the shells of creatures that had lived in the sea, was quickly weathered away, exposing the granite. But the earth movements that exposed the land, and the activity that created the

granite, meant that the granite was not exposed in a continuous sheet but as a series of lumps. There are four lumps in Cornwall – the one that forms Bodmin Moor is the most famous – and off Land's End the Isles of Scilly are another. The largest granite lump lies in Devon. This is Dartmoor.

The M5 motorway ends at Exeter, the county town of Devon. At the motorway's end the traveller is offered a choice of routes, either following the A38 towards Plymouth and the holiday resorts of Torbay and south Devon, or the A30 towards Okehampton, and the resorts of north Devon and Cornwall. The routes of these two holiday roads

Above: Porch doorway: Corndon Ford farm
Left: Stuart Arthur thatching at Ponsworthy

are defined as much by geography as by the areas they serve. To the west of Exeter lies Dartmoor and though roads do cross the high moor the main routes have always crossed the lowlands at the moor's edge. The A38 runs along the southern side of the moor, defining the Dartmoor National Park along part of its journey, while the A30 follows the northern edge. Dartmoor covers 368 square miles (954 sq km), almost filling Devon between Exeter and the Cornish border and stretching south to within a dozen kilometres of the coast. Only north Devon and the small part of the county east of the M5 is not dominated by the moor.

Two B roads – the B3212 and B3357 – cross the moor from east to west, intersecting at Two Bridges and dividing the highest land into four uneven parts. To the north is highest Dartmoor, rising to 2,039ft (619m) on High Willhays. High Willhays is often described as the highest point in England south of Kinder Scout, but there is actually higher ground on the Herefordshire side of the eastern Black Mountains ridge on the Welsh border: perhaps it could be said that Dartmoor's peak is the highest wholly English mountain south of the Peak

Looking up Moor Brook towards
West Mill Tor and Yes Tor

District. Close to High Willhays are a series of other, sometimes more distinctive, peaks.

To the south of the two B roads is truly wild country, a barren landscape with
fewer, and lower, distinctive tops, a land for the connoisseur of wilderness qualities. To the west the intersecting roads create a small triangle of moor on which
some of Dartmoor's best prehistoric sites are to be found. Eastwards the roads
create a larger triangle in which sits Widecombe-in-the-Moor, Dartmoor's most
famous village. There are other villages, too, the moor here being a gentler place.

Dartmoor is a raised plateau of granite, high enough for the peninsula's prevailing south-westerly winds to sweep across it at gale force. High enough, too,
to attract the clouds rolling in from the Atlantic. In summer the clouds bring a
drenching rain, in winter there can be snow lying on the moor even though the
Devon coasts are usually snow, and even frost, free. On highest Dartmoor, the
poor acidic soil that is formed from weathered granite and decomposed and
decomposing vegetation, combined with wind, rain and cold, means that livestock need to be hardy, and that crop growing is all but impossible. The result
is a huge area of virtually 'undisturbed' moorland, a rare habitat for wildlife,
and with many prehistoric monuments which have avoided being ploughed,
their fate in more fertile parts of the country. It was in part to protect this
moorland that Dartmoor was given National Park status in October 1951, the
fourth Park to be designated, and still the most southerly of the National Parks
of England and Wales.

Dartmoor has an annual rainfall of over 60in (around 150cm), rather more
falling on the western moorland edge which first sees the Atlantic's clouds. This

rain, together with the thin acidic soil, which favours the production of peat, aids the creation of bog. In popular imagination Dartmoor is most famous for its bogs, fame enhanced by Conan Doyle's *The Hound of the Baskervilles*, though the moor was famous – perhaps that should be infamous – as a place of leg-devouring bogs long before Conan Doyle moved Sherlock Holmes from Baker Street to Grimpen Mire. In 1586 William Campden referred to *squalida montana, Dartmore*, a phrase that is more descriptive for not needing translation. Then, most famously, the Rev Sabine Baring-Gould noted in his *Book of Dartmoor* – published in 1900 and still on the compulsory reading list for lovers of the moor – the comment of a Plymouth tailor: 'I solemnly swear to you, Sir, nothing will ever induce me to set foot on Dartmoor again. If I chance to see it from the Hoe, Sir, I'll avert my eyes. How can people think to come here for pleasure – for pleasure, Sir! – only unwholesome-minded individuals can love Dartmoor.'

Those that walk the moorland of north and south Dartmoor would doubtless object to being classified as 'unwholesome-minded'! The very things which repelled the Plymouth tailor are the moor's attraction to those who venture deep into it. True, the country is uncompromising – almost every Dartmoor walker has a tale of firm-looking ground that turned out to be a quaker, of a bog that suddenly decided it preferred to be inside rather than outside a boot, or of a mist that crept up quietly, but quickly, shrouding the moor and disorientating the mind. But to the lover of the moor the mists offer the chance of a better understanding of map and compass, the occasional wet day the chance of adding to a fund of stories of days on the moor. On other walks – on most walks – the moor will be

Yellowmead quadruple stone circle

gentle, the heather in full purple, the rivers sparkling, the views panoramic and the walking magnificent.

Of course, not everyone visits the moor equipped or inclined to venture into its empty heart. Such visitors are equally well satisfied. Where Dartmoor's granite has been exposed to the elements it has been weathered into fantastic shapes, known by the local name of tor. Many of the finest tors lie within easy reach of car parks and bus stops, particularly on the eastern moor where Haytor, Hound Tor, Bowerman's Nose – to name only the most famous – are just short walks from the roadside. Such tors often form the basis of local legends which make a visit even more entertaining, none more so than Vixen Tor on the western moor with its legend of a flesh-devouring witch.

Though the same geology creates both, the contrast between the hard, angular tors and the Dartmoor bogs could hardly be greater. But visitors surprised by that contrast will be even more surprised if they visit sites on the rim of the National Park. East of the A382 in the valley of the River Teign and west of the A386 in the Lyd's valley are exquisite sections of broadleaved woodland, the woodland floor a haven for wild flowers, the trees home to a wholly different range of birds to those seen on the high moorland. Neither are these stretches of beautiful woodland isolated examples. Close to the A38 the valley of the River Bovey is more extensively wooded than either the Lyd or the Teign; there is fine woodland in the River Plym's valley near Shaugh Prior; and, most significantly of all, the Dart valley is heavily wooded – both broadleaved and mixed forests – along much of its length from Dartmeet to the National Park's border.

Dartmeet is where the East and West Dart Rivers join, each having risen on the northern moor. Many contend, and with good reason, that the Dart is the loveliest of all English rivers. The river

Above: Winter stands still on the East Okement river

Left: Teignhead clapper bridge. The origins of Dartmoor's clapper bridges are shrouded in mystery – even the name. Many have suggested a Roman origin, but there is scant evidence for this

Scorhill stone circle in winter, looking towards Cosdon Beacon

Pages 14–15: Bonehill, Widecombe-in-the-Moor. Early farmers needed to clear the clitter of granite slabs and boulders which covered the moor, making a virtue of the necessity by building their farms and walls from it. The granite produced buildings strong enough to withstand the elements, and which now enhance many moorland views

also names the moor, an appropriate choice in view of its beauty and popularity. But the Dart is not the only Dartmoor river. The raised granite plateau is the mother of rivers. Here, too, rise the Teign which reaches the sea at Teignmouth, and the Tavy, which names Tavistock and flows into the Tamar on the outskirts of Plymouth.

Dartmeet is one of the beauty spots on Dartmoor, a visitor attraction in the conventional sense. The Lydford Gorge – the tight valley of the River Lyd – is another, as are the Teign Valley and Lustleigh Cleave, the gorge on the River Bovey. Dartmoor also has waterfalls, notably White Lady Falls in Lydford Gorge and Becky Falls near Manaton; majestic panoramas from well-known viewpoints and prehistoric sites to intrigue the visitors – Dartmoor has the largest concentration of Bronze Age sites in the country. It also has Buckfast Abbey, a still-occupied monastery, and Castle Drogo, a National Trust property. Some visitors even find a grim fascination in the prison at Princetown.

Some 30,000 people live within the National Park, 1 in 8 of them in Ashburton, the Park's largest town, the rest in a scattering of villages, chiefly around the edge and on the western moor. Of the villages the most famous is Widecombe-in-the-Moor which justifies the extension to its name by nestling in the moorland folds to the west of Haytor. It is hard to escape Uncle Tom Cobley and all at

Widecombe, but behind the old folk song is a very attractive village with a fine church. Lovers of old villages and churches will not be disappointed on Dartmoor: besides Widecombe-in-the-Moor there are other delightful places – Lustleigh, Buckland-in-the-Moor, and Meavy and Sheepstor both close to Burrator Reservoir, and Belstone at the northern edge of the National Park. Equally fascinating is Moretonhampstead, the old market town in the north-east of the Park. The villages and market towns mainly grew from farming interests on the moor and the moorland fringe. There was also exploitation of the mineral wealth locked up in the rocks, and of the rock itself. Of this, the chief reminders are the ruins of a tinworking industry which dot the moor, though china clay is still extracted in the south of the National Park and granite has been quarried at Merrivale until very recently. The future of the quarry remains uncertain.

Farming is still the main occupation of those who live within the National Park, though the number of farms has been declining steadily for many years. The high moor is a harsh place, even for sheep bred to withstand the rigours of winter. Visitors will also see fewer of the moor's famous ponies now, mechanisation of coal mines and the absence of European Union subsidies on them making their breeding a difficult business.

The ponies and sheep that remain graze the common land at the moor's heart. Ironically, the difficult conditions of the commons for farming has ensured their survival, attempts at enclosure having failed. The result is superb access for the visitor, walkers and horse riders being allowed to explore the 40 per cent of the National Park that is registered as common, as well as exploring other access areas and following several hundred kilometres of footpaths elsewhere.

On the northern moor access is restricted at certain times by the Ministry of Defence's use for live firing. In practice live firing is limited, access being allowed at times most visitors will find convenient – weekends, public holidays and summer months. However, walkers are warned not to touch metal objects they come across, a fact which fuels the debate on the suitability of a National Park for such activity. The debate is not clear-cut – does the existence of such ranges offer more protection than destruction to the landscape, acting as a barrier against commercial exploitation?

There are considerable economic benefits from the MoD's presence on the moor, brought about by the national need for defence training. Currently about 100,000 military personnel come to Dartmoor to train every year.

Against this have to be balanced (a) the restrictions to public access and implications for public safety, (b) the disturbance to wildlife and (c) the visual intrusion of tracks, look-outs and all the other impedimenta of the military in tracts of wild country.

On days when the red flags are not flying, visitors exploring the northern moor might like to debate the issue more fully.

Hamel Down has many ancient cairns and barrows, all built of local granite. Beside the ancient cairn on Hameldown Tor is a much newer man-made marker, an Ordnance Survey trig point in concrete

I The rocks beneath: geology and scenery

The first-time visitor to the National Park often carries a mental picture of Dartmoor. If that picture's source is Grimpen Mire, the formidable bog that confronted Sherlock Holmes in *The Hound of the Baskervilles*, then the visitor expects a bleak, boggy wilderness. If, instead, it is the moorland of picture postcards, then the expectation is the purple sea of a classic heather moor.

Each of these pictures is, of course, a clichéd view of the National Park, as are the ideas that Dartmoor is peppered with a whole series of quaint villages, just like Widecombe-in-the-Moor, peopled by Uncle Tom Cobley and all, or that it is a grassy upland on which ponies roam.

But, as with all clichés, there is truth behind the stereotypes. The first-time visitor following one of the roads that bisects the moor may glimpse all these aspects of the moor, but may also be astonished at the number of other Dartmoors that can be seen – the farmland and luxuriously-wooded valleys at the moorland rim; the beautiful rivers; the tors and litter of granite blocks on the hillsides.

For some visitors part of the astonishment is that the granite which lies beneath the National Park is capable of forming the basis of such a range of scenery. Granite does indeed create more than one scenic form, but granite lies beneath only 65 per cent of the National Park – the upland heart of Dartmoor – the surrounding rim comprising other rock types which contribute to the scenic diversity.

View from Holwell Tor looking towards Greator Rocks and Hound Tor

GRANITE AND THE ICE AGES

Dartmoor's granite flowed as a molten rock from deep within the earth into the roots of the Cornubian Mountains which stretched along the south-west peninsula at that time, some 280 million years ago. The granite intrusion created a single mass of rock known as a batholith, and a number of thickened bosses formed along its length. These bosses are the granite outcrops of Devon and Cornwall. Dartmoor is the largest and most easterly of the outcrops: to the west are Bodmin Moor, the outcrops of St Austell and Carnmenillis, Penwith Moor near Land's End and the Isles of Scilly.

As the granite cooled it shrank and the shrinkage – perhaps aided by pressure from below – created a series of vertical and horizontal joints in the solid rock. When the rocks above the granite had weathered away, by about 75 million years ago, the exposed granite was attacked by the elements. Though granite is inherently tough – it is one of nature's densest, hardest rocks – it is surprisingly vulnerable chemically. Rainwater, which is slightly acidic because of dissolved carbon dioxide, attacks the minerals that form the granite, breaking down biotite into a red-brown slurry which occasionally stains the rock. China clay, which occurs as large deposits on south-west Dartmoor resulted from the decomposition of feldspar crystals during the granite's emplacement and cooling. Quartz is a much more resistant mineral, and the gravel (called *growan* by locals) that washes out after the feldspar and biotite disintegrate, is composed mainly of quartz crystals.

Rain is not the only weathering agent of the granite. As everyone who has suffered a burst pipe knows, the freezing and thawing of water can have a major effect. Although burst pipes are only noticed when the ice thaws, it is actually the

The moor's granite clitter occasionally included slabs conveniently sized for gateposts. The ones shown here frame the view of Vixen Tor beyond the Walkham valley

GRANITE

*Granite is essentially composed of three minerals –
quartz, feldspar and mica. Quartz is silicone
dioxide: in its purest form the mineral is clear and
colourless (and called rock crystal), but on
Dartmoor quartz crystals are normally milky, or
even grey. Feldspar exists in two forms, orthoclase
and plagioclase. Orthoclase is potassium aluminium
silicate and is white or even pinkish; plagioclase is a
more complex mixture of calcium, sodium and
aluminium silicates and is greyish-white. Mica also
comes in several forms, but on Dartmoor the usual
form is biotite, a grey-black mixture of magnesium,
iron, potassium, aluminium and hydrogen silicate. In
addition to the three main minerals Dartmoor
granite also has smaller quantities of tourmaline, a
mixture of boron and aluminium silicate, and some
alkalis. Tourmaline is black.*

*The size of the crystals of these minerals
depends on the cooling rate of the liquid rock. In
general the granite of the exposed tors is coarse-
grained (ie has large crystals), a fact which partly
contributed to their survival when quarrymen came
to exploit Dartmoor's rock. Just below the surface,
and easily reached, was a finer-grained rock, a
much better quality building stone.*

*Geologists recognise various forms of granite on
Dartmoor. Contact granite includes fragments of the
sedimentary rocks into which the liquid rock
intruded. Tor granite is coarse grained and has large
crystals of feldspar. Below it lies the finer-grained
aplogranite. A fourth form, known as blue granite, is
a form of aplogranite created by a liquid rock
intrusion into the existing granite batholith.
Consequently it lies below the surface, though it can
be seen at the base of the western outcrop of
Haytor (an outcrop known as Low Man).*

*As the granite cooled, not only did mineral
crystals form, but by a chemical process known as
pneumatolysis metallic ores were created. Tin has
been the most commercially important ore to have
been worked on Dartmoor, though copper, lead and
arsenic have also been mined, and zinc, tungsten,
cobalt, uranium and even gold exist in small, non-
commercially viable, quantities.*

*The layered nature of much of Dartmoor's granite
– a structure which aided tor formation – is well
shown at Watern Tor*

water freezing which does the damage. Water expands on freezing producing a local pressure in any constriction that can be more than a hundred times normal atmospheric pressure. The process works just as well on rock as it does on water pipes, as water freezes in cracks in the rock and levers the granite blocks apart. This process continues today during the regular freeze-thaws of winter, but was at its most significant during the Ice Ages.

Dartmoor was never glaciated, but lay in the periglacial fringe, the area south of the permanent ice sheets and glaciers, where the soil and rocks were deep frozen for much of the time, but subjected to regular summer thaws. Such deep frosts and thaws would have accelerated the weathering process, levering off huge blocks of granite from the exposed tors. The weathering of the tor granite by rain and ice helped to create the fantastic shapes of some of the rock features, such as Bowerman's Nose and rock castles such as Hound Tor. Occasionally the weathering detached a block from the one below leaving it so well balanced that the upper stone would rock gently under the slightest pressure. Dartmoor has several of these 'logan' rocks, some whose rocking was so delicate they could be used to crack nuts. The name logan derives from logging, the old word for rocking: anciently it was said that the rocking foretold the future to anyone wise enough to interpret the movement.

The piles of granite blocks which litter the summits and flanks of some of Dartmoor's peaks, a by-product of the weathering process, caused geologists a problem for many years. Just how did weathering of the tors manage to throw vast granite blocks such large distances? The answer lies back in the Ice Ages when the regular thawing of the top few centimetres of soil created a muddy, slippery layer on top of the frozen sub-soil, known as permafrost. Rainwater, unable to penetrate the permafrost, ran off downhill, taking the muddy layer with it in a process geologists have given the delightful name of 'congelifluction'. This surface movement is capable of carrying large granite blocks with it, distributing the demolished tor across the hillside. The jumble of granite blocks is known locally as *clitter*. Congelifluction also smoothes out the irregularities on hillsides and valley floors, creating the scene we see today, with the tors standing above a smooth, well-rounded landscape.

The periglacial conditions on Dartmoor during the last Ice Ages also created a curious network of almost symmetrical features – circles, polygons and stripes – on the ground as the constant freezing and thawing 'sorts' stones and small boulders. Such areas of 'patterned ground' can be seen above Merrivale Quarry, in the Meavy valley above Burrator Reservoir and near Leedon Tor.

AFTER THE ICE AGES

When the ice retreated, plants from the south established themselves on the moor. Granite produces a poor, acidic soil, but despite this a small range of plants thrives. Pollen analysis has shown that juniper and dwarf varieties of birch and willow, together with some pine, soon became established. These plants fertilised the soil and when the climate improved significantly, oak, elm and hazel colonised the moor. The extent to which Britain was forested before Man began to clear the trees to cultivate the land is still debated by experts, but on Dartmoor it seems that the tree cover was total or, at least, extensive up to the 450m (about 1,500ft) contour. Above that the moor was typical heathland, with a scattering of shrubs and small trees.

Prehistoric man, who cleared the forests, may have grown cereals on the exposed fertile land, but the transition of the soil to podzol meant that very soon the moor was only good for rough grazing. Sheep nibbled the shoots of trees and shrubs attempting to re-establish themselves, and in a relatively short time the

ROCK BASINS

As well as engineering the destruction of the tors, freeze-thawing can have more local effects. The cooling of the liquid rocks occasionally causes relatively thin layers of horizontal rock to be formed. Ice penetrating the cracks between these layers can lever them apart, or loosen individual crystals, to create a shallow hollow in the rock. The hollow fills with rainwater and rock particles and the swirling action of wind can undercut the pool edges, assisting the freeze-thawing in creating a rock basin. Such basins are frequently circular, leading to the early view that they were carved by human hands rather than by the forces of nature. Consequently legends arose of their being Druidic vessels constructed to catch the blood of sacrificial victims. Good rock basins can be seen on Great Mis Tor and Kes Tor.

An extreme form of rock basin is created by flowing water, as can be seen in the Cauldron in Lydford Gorge, where the swirling waters of the Lyd has carved deep, smooth-sided bowls out of the bedrock. A similar process created the famous Tolmen (holed stone) near the Teign-a-ver clapper bridge (opposite). In local folklore, crawling through the hole cured rheumatism.

PEAT FORMATION

The cutting of the trees by the first moorland farmers seems to have more or less coincided with a worsening of the climate, the temperature dropping and rainfall increasing. Granite is impervious, and the increased rain caused the moorland soil to become waterlogged, despite the well-developed river systems. The decay of vegetation requires oxygen and bacteria, but the water excluded oxygen and leached acid from the underlying rock, inhibiting bacterial growth. The result was that dead plant material, particularly sphagnum moss, did not decompose, instead forming a brown, mud-like layer – peat. The peat now underlies the famous upland and valley bogs of Dartmoor. On the hillsides the run-off of the increased rainfall carried away the nutrients leaving behind a grey soil called podzol (from the Russian word for ash as the soil's colour resembles that of wood ash).

Will Webber and Norman Mortimore cutting peat on Gidleigh Common

moor we see today was established. Only in three places – Wistman's Wood in the West Dart valley near Two Bridges; Black Tor Copse in the West Okement valley, and Piles Copse in the Erme valley – have areas of upland woodland survived. In these locations the oaks have remained ungrazed because the clitter among which they grow makes access difficult for sheep. Apart from these copses, and the occasional hardy, wind-thrashed trees that can be found nestling in unlikely but equally well-protected places, the upland moor is an undulating landscape of rough grasses and heathers, interspersed with areas of bog.

RAIN AND RIVERS

The high moorland plateau of Dartmoor intercepts the prevailing south-westerly winds that reach Britain from the Atlantic, laden with moisture from their sweep across the ocean. The plateau forces the air to rise and cool, causing clouds to form and rain to fall. Such an effect does Dartmoor have that Exeter, to the east of the moor and in the classical 'rain-shadow' position, receives only one-fifth the amount of rain that falls on Princetown. Even on the moor such rain-shadowing is noticeable, with the rainfall dropping off significantly to the east of the high moor. The rain is absorbed by the bogs, which act as a giant sponge, slowing down the rate of water release into the moorland rivers.

Not surprisingly, the moor has been and continues to be an important source of water supply, whether directly from streams, springs and wells, or indirectly via leats and pipes. Leats (channels dug from the moor) originally conveyed water to farms and villages, but later to towns further away. In 1585 an Act of Parliament gave the city of Plymouth permission to 'digge a Trenche through and over all the landes and groundes lying between Plymouth and anye parts of the said river of Mew'. This work, which created the most celebrated of Dartmoor's leats, was carried out under the direction of Sir Francis Drake. Drake's Leat linked the River Meavy ('Mew' is an eccentric, Elizabethan spelling of the name) to the city and can still be followed for much of its length from the dam of Burrator Reservoir, which now fills part of the Meavy valley. As an aside here, some 200 years later, Drake's Leat allowed an insight into the character of Dr Samuel Johnson, the great man of letters. In 1762 Johnson visited Plymouth with Sir Joshua Reynolds at a time when there was a heated debate over whether the expanding new dockyard town of Devonport should be allowed to share the Dartmoor water supplied by Drake's channel. Johnson immediately sided with the old city against the upstart 'dockers' declaring: 'Let them die of thirst, they shall not have a drop', his innate conservatism over-riding his compassion. It is doubtful whether Johnson's view carried any weight, for eventually a second channel, the Devonport Leat, was cut. It, too, can still be followed.

The Dartmoor leats, some cut to supply water to power waterwheels associated with tinworkings, are occasionally useful as guides across the moor, especially in its south-western corner. Rivers are equally useful, and have the extra advantage of offering a quite different scenic aspect of the high moor. The moorland plateau is not flat, but slightly tilted, the highest peaks lying near the northern edge, from where the moor slopes gently southwards. As a rule, most rivers which drain the high moor therefore flow south. The Dart begins as two separate streams – and a host of tributaries (some experts claim over fifty) – rising to the south of Cranmere Pool and joining at Dartmeet. Here the deep, sheltered valleys of the twin and combined rivers have allowed trees and taller shrubs to flourish, a striking contrast to the barren upland where the rivers rise. The rivers Bovey, Avon, Erme and Plym all flow south from the moor, the

Above: Sheepstor village and Burrator Reservoir

Left: Devonport Leat was built when the demand for water at the new naval dockyard outstripped the capacity of the leat built by Sir Francis Drake to supply Plymouth. Devonport Leat can still be followed across the moor

Overleaf: Wistman's Wood: one of only three surviving areas of upland oak wood on the moor, providing a rare habitat for lichens, mosses and wildlife

The River Webburn, which flows through the Widecombe valley, joins the River Dart at Buckland Bridge

Walkham and the Tavy, which drain the western moor, flowing west down the plateau edge before turning south towards the sea.

The Tavy offers a complete contrast to the lush Dart valley, echoing the wilderness of the high moor. As it descends the steep moorland edge the river flows through a deep, steep-sided, barren gorge (a feature known locally as a cleave, though that word originally meant the cliff in the valley side rather than the gorge itself). The Tavy rises close to the West Dart, the two rivers lying on opposite sides of the high moor's east-west watershed. In a distance of only about 6 miles (10km), the Tavy falls over 980ft (300m), the water galloping down this impressively-steep course having exploited jointing in the granite to cut a deep gorge into which clitter from the surrounding tors has spilled. The rushing water, with occasional short waterfalls over granite steps, the litter of granite blocks, and the fact that the cleave is tree-less give it a marvellously wild atmosphere.

Just as the east-west watershed separates the West Dart and Tavy sources, the north-south Dartmoor watershed (which lies very close to Cranmere Pool) separates East Dart Head from Taw Head, the two sources again being just a few tens of metres apart. The Taw flows north, but the high northern rim of the moor ensures that this direction of flow cannot be reversed, the river continuing northwards to reach Devon's Atlantic Coast. The twin Okement rivers also head north from the western side of the north moors. The other famous Dartmoor river, the Teign, also rises close to East Dart Head, flowing east before turning south for the English Channel coast.

As it leaves the moor, the Teign also flows in a tight gorge. But rather than treeless and rugged, the Teign's gorge is deeply wooded, an exquisitely-beautiful section of country, a 'soft' landscape after the harshness of the upland moor where the river rises. The reason for this change of scenery, and that of the lower Dart valley, and of the Lydford Gorge, so famously beautiful it has been brought by the National Trust and preserved as part of the English heritage, is a change in the underlying rock.

THE COUNTRY ROCKS

The Dartmoor granite was intruded into an existing rock mass – called the 'country rocks' by geologists. The searing heat of the liquid granite baked the country rocks for up to 4 miles (6km) from the intrusion edge and, through a variety of chemical processes, changed their structure. This change of state is called metamorphosis, the ring of metamorphosed rock around the granite boss being called

View across Vellake Corner: the West Okement river feeding Meldon Reservoir

FOSSILS AND CAVES

Finally, in this overview of the main geographical aspects of the National Park one surprising aspect must be mentioned. At the south-eastern edge of the Park, near Buckfastleigh, there is a small area of Carboniferous limestone. This particular form of limestone dissolves in rainwater (because of acidity of the rain), the water eating its way along fault lines in the rock.

Over the last 150,000 years, rain and streams created cave systems in the rock. Near Buckfastleigh, quarrying for limestone cut into several caves in which were found the fossilised remains of lion, hippopotamus, hyena and elephant. It is thought that the bones of the animals had been washed into the caves, rather than the animals having fallen into or been trapped in the caves. These fossils make the caves one of the most important sites of their period in Britain.

The caves also contain good flowstone (stalagmite and stalactite) formations. In one a stalagmite boss in the shape of a man was found. As the base stood almost directly below the tomb of Squire Richard Cabell in Buckfastleigh church, it is speculated that the discovery started, or reinforced, the legend of the evil squire. One of the Buckfastleigh caves is occasionally open to the public.

an aureole. Within this aureole, the country rocks closest to the granite have been transformed into *hornfels*, a flinty rock containing minerals from both the granite and the original rock, and marbles, the polished form of metamorphosed limestone. Away from the aureole, the country rocks of the Carboniferous period, into which the magma intruded, remain intact.

The National Park includes much of the metamorphic aureole and sections of the original country rocks, particularly on the eastern and western sides of the moor. This extension of the National Park beyond the granite boundary means that the wooded valleys of the Teign and Dart and the Lydford Gorge are included, as are the equally beautiful wooded valleys of the Plym and the Bovey. The former, near Shaugh Prior, is superb and includes the Dewerstone, a distinctive granite lump around which one of Dartmoor's more brutal folk tales is wound. Close to Bovey Tracey, the River Bovey flows through the equally attractive Lustleigh Cleave. Nearby, a tributary of the Bovey cascades over Becky Falls. Interestingly, one of the National Park's most famous landmarks, the church-topped Brent Tor, also lies beyond the granite boundary. Many visitors imagine that the tor is granite, but it is in fact basaltic lava and represents another igneous intrusion.

The lower lands of the National Park, which lie between the wooded river valleys of the periphery, offer a further scenic contrast. Here the patchwork of fields allows rugged upland Dartmoor to blend seamlessly with the traditional Devon of the cream teas.

Dartmoor has no natural lakes, though the walker does occasionally come across small pools in natural or man-excavated hollows. Ironically, the most famous such pool, Cranmere, is no longer permanently water-filled. There are, however, eight large bodies of water within the National Park boundaries, all of them reservoirs, the earliest constructed in the 1860s. Dartmoor's enthusiasm for collecting rain made it an obvious place to site reservoirs once the population centres of Devon had outgrown the ability of leats to supply them, and increased awareness of public health had made them an impractical source of water. The first reservoir was Tottiford, later extended by the creation of the Kennick and Trenchford Reservoirs. Both here and at Burrator, completed in the 1890s, the water is surrounded by extensive conifer plantations (the one-time prevailing view being that such plantations somehow attracted rain). Such plantations add little to the scenery of the high moor, but they do make an attractive backdrop to the reservoirs, as well as offering a habitat to unusual species of birds. The later Dartmoor reservoirs are not similarly cloaked, giving them a more natural look. However, the construction of such bodies of water within a National Park has been controversial. While Dartmoor, as an area of high rainfall, would seem to be ideally suited for reservoirs, the creation of National Parks was designed to protect wild landscapes and habitats. There was a major debate before the Meldon dam was built, and the Meldon reservoir was the last to have been built – in 1972 – within the National Park. All the Dartmoor reservoirs are controlled by South West Water and are stocked with trout. Details on permits to fish the reservoirs can be obtained from the address given at the end of the book.

Opposite: (top) The Dart valley and Luckey Tor; (below) whatever the arguments for and against the construction of the Meldon dam and reservoir within the National Park, the statistics of the system are impressive. The dam is 200m long and 44m high. It required 270,000 tons of concrete and holds back 300 million litres (nearly 80 million gallons) of water. The surface area of the reservoir is 60 acres (about 25 hectares)

2 Climate, vegetation and wildlife

An old Dartmoor saying maintains that the moor has nine months of winter and three months of bad weather. If that sounds unduly pessimistic it is worth remembering a moorland rhyme which relates the likely weather to the wind direction:

The south wind blows and brings wet weather
The north gives wet and cold together
The west wind comes brimful of rain
The east wind drives it back again

Widecombe church is often called the 'Cathedral of the Moor' because of its size and the splendour of its pinnacled tower. The tower was probably built in the late fifteenth or early sixteenth century and is 135ft (41m) high. The church is dedicated to St Pancras

Dartmoor folk might be hardy, but when it comes to moorland weather they seem determined to take a gloomy view.

The reality, of course, is that a gloomy view could often be used as a description of Dartmoor. The moor's position means it intercepts Britain's prevailing south-westerlies as they sweep in from the Atlantic. The moisture-ladened air is forced upwards by the moor, cooling as it rises and so forming clouds. On average

The edge of the blanket bog at the headwaters of the Cherry Brook

2.1m (that's 82in, almost 7ft) of rain falls on Princetown each year. The wettest month is December, but no month escapes the rain: the average July rainfall is half that of December, and even the driest months (April and May) have around 40 per cent of December's total. Because of the way the clouds form, most of the rain falls on the high moor. On the National Park's western fringe the annual rainfall is around 47in (1.2m), and is even lower on Dartmoor's rain-shadowed eastern edge. It is also occasionally the case that even on rain-free days the moor is enveloped in low cloud or mist, usually a cold, damp mist that blocks out the sun.

Dartmoor can also be a cold place, with minimum recorded winter temperatures below –10 degrees C in Princetown, implying very cold days on the high moor. With no surrounding high ground to absorb the punishing winds, in either winter and summer, such tall shrub and trees that do gain a foothold on the high moor grow into stunted specimens which twist dramatically away from the wind in an effort to escape its chilling effect.

However, the 'English Riviera' with its palm trees and sunbathing crowds is just a few miles to the south, proof that, in British terms, Devon has an enviable climate. The sheltered valleys of the high moor and the lower areas of the moorland rim are therefore warm and well-watered, ideal conditions for plant growth. This unusual combination of a damp, cold upland with a warm, but moist, fringe attracts a remarkable mixture of plants and animals, particularly birds. Dartmoor is the southern limit for several northern species, while the sheltered valleys of the eastern fringe of the National Park are close to the northern limit of some southern species. This combination, and the wide range of habitats, makes the moor one of Britain's most important wildlife areas.

BLANKET BOG

As noted in Chapter 1 on Dartmoor's geology and scenery, the upland combination of rainfall and granite has created a waterlogged, acidic soil and a consequent covering of peat. The peat underlies the blanket bog, a generic term for an area which occupies about 15 per cent of the area of the National Park and covers highest Dartmoor. There are actually two large areas of blanket bog covering the

upland areas of the northern and southern moors, representing about 35 per cent of the unenclosed moorland. Despite the size of the Dartmoor blanket bogs, the moor represents only a small fraction of British bogs. But as it is the most southerly in Britain, and British bogs are a sizeable percentage of the world's acreage, Dartmoor is an important site and has been recognised as a priority conservation habitat by the European Union.

The peat underlying the bog is rarely less than 20in (50cm) thick and frequently extends for several yards. Over the years, peat has been cut from the moor and fires have also reduced its coverage. The use of the northern moor for live-firing, particularly the past use of heavy weapons has also created craters which have aided natural erosion. To these human effects is added a natural decline in the bog, for reasons not well understood, although there is some evidence that acid rain has been influential. The decline can be most readily seen in the creation of peat hags, 'mushrooms' of peat separated by deep channels as the peat mass shrinks.

This decline in the moor's blanket bog is important for two reason. Firstly the bog is a natural sponge, absorbing rainwater and then acting as a regulator as it releases it into the moorland rivers. A reduction in bog coverage may increase rainwater run-off and consequently increase the likelihood of flash flooding of the rivers. Because of the prevailing south-westerly winds, flash flooding of rivers draining the local moors has always been a problem. On 17 August 1917, rain increased the flow of the Red-a-Ven Brook, which flows north from near High Willhays, by an estimated 4,000 times, and boulders weighing several tons were carried downhill by the torrent. More recently, in August 1952, a similar flash flood of Exmoor's River Lyn devastated the village of Lynmouth and killed thirty-four people.

Above: Looking towards Haytor from Greator Rocks

Right: Cotton grass. In spring its bright yellow anthers may confuse some visitors, but the fluffy white cottonheads of summer are unmistakable

Far left: Stonecrop
Centre left: Dartmoor is the southern breeding limit of the golden plover and also an important winter habitat (Mark Hamblin)
Left: Bright yellow tormentil

BEWARE OF BOGS

As young and quite inexperienced walkers, a friend and I ventured on to the southern moor and, looking for a place to rest, made for an attractively emerald green section of ground. The bootfulls of liquid peat mud were an immediate (and long-lasting) lesson in Dartmoor geography.

I was grateful to learn that we were not the first to have been tempted by a valley mire, the occasionally-used names of 'featherbed' or 'quaker' for the bogs – because of the way in which they quake underfoot as they are crossed – suggest Man's long acquaintance. Tales of people drowning in valley bogs are probably exaggerations, though some experts believe that ponies may have occasionally been engulfed, their long spindly legs being poorly designed for dragging them clear. One famous Dartmoor story tells of a walker who saw a top hat at the centre of a 'quaker'. Gingerly, the man edged across the bog and lifted the hat. To his astonishment there was a head underneath, its owner promptly asking for assistance in getting free. Regaining his composure, the rescuer asked where he should attach a rope for hauling and was told that it might be best if it were fastened to the horse on which he was sat. The story gives an idea of the fearsome reputation that grew up around some valley bogs, a reputation that almost certainly led Arthur Conan Doyle to set The Hound of the Baskervilles *on the moor. It is widely believed that Foxtor Mires, on the southern moor, was the model for Grimpen Mire.*

The second reason for concern over the decline in blanket bog is the loss of wildlife habitat. The bog moss *Sphagnum imbricatum* was a main peat forming plant, but is now restricted to two sites on the moor. Dartmoor is also the southern limit of crowberry, an evergreen mat-forming shrub with berries which are green at first, before turning pale purple and, finally, a distinctive black.

Blanket bog is composed chiefly of what are known generically as bog mosses, mostly forms of sphagnum together with rushes and sedges, but is also home to clumps of deer grass and, especially on the southern moor, purple moorgrass. On the drier sections of the bog, ling and cross-leaved heath thrive and walkers may find patches of bilberry. Diligent plant lovers may also find tormentil and the blue-flowered milkwort. In the wetter areas, most walkers will see cotton-grass (both common and hare's tail can be found on the moor) with its distinctive fluffy, white seed heads and, perhaps, more exotic flowers including the insectivorous common sundew and bog asphodel with its bright orange, starred flowers.

The bog is home to few birds, and such species as do occur are unfortunately diminishing in number. Golden plover and dunlin both nest on the moor, in each case at the southern limit of their range. The golden plover also over-winters, occasionally forming large flocks. The moor's dunlin population is of international importance, as numbers are declining throughout Europe.

One particular form of blanket bog must also be mentioned. To the east of Princetown lies the Tor Royal bog, a 19-acre (8ha) 'raised bog' where the peat deposit forms a raised dome. Tor Royal is the only raised bog on the south-west peninsula, and again is of international importance as it is largely untouched.

VALLEY BOGS

Blanket bog forms on upland plateaux and hillsides, water draining from them in the numerous streams which form Dartmoor's rivers. In the valley bottoms, particularly where the rivers themselves are slow-flowing and the valleys are flat-bottomed, the ground on each bank of the river becomes waterlogged. Here considerable depths of peat are created, and a habitat quite different from the upland bogs is being formed.

Because of the unique circumstances which give rise to valley bogs (or 'mires' as they are known locally), the area of such bogs is less than 10 per cent of that covered by blanket bog. But despite this relatively small acreage, Dartmoor (and nearby Bodmin Moor) has the finest examples of the type in Britain. The bogs are also of international importance. The characteristic plant of the bogs is sphagnum, which often forms an alluring bright green covering to the very liquid mire.

Sphagnum moss has remarkable water-retaining properties, and was used as a dressing in the 1914–18 war, as an early nappy and, today, as the basis of hanging baskets (not utilising moss derived from Dartmoor's bogs). But though it is the characteristic plant, the bogs are home to a large number of other water-loving plants. Common cotton-grass, bog asphodel and common sundew are found here as well as in the blanket bogs, as are the pink-flowered bog pimpernel, bogbean, water crowfoot, marsh St John's wort with its delicate yellow-trumpet flowers, and the equally delicate white flowers of pale butterwort. Rarer flowers include oblong-leaved sundew, as with its cousin an insectivorous species, marsh louse-wort, its pretty red/pink snapdragon-like flowers belying its name, and the tall bog myrtle. The real rarities of the Dartmoor valley bogs are bog orchid and Irish lady's tresses. The thin stems and yellow-green flowers of bog orchid are very dif-

ficult to spot among the sphagnum, and the plant is threatened throughout its European range. Irish lady's tresses is also an orchid, with a white, trumpet-like flower. Outside Ireland and Scotland, it is known at only one site on Dartmoor.

As might be expected, the valley bogs are home to frogs, and also to several species of rare dragonflies and damsel-flies. Dartmoor is of national importance for its population of the keeled skimmer dragonfly, a beautiful species with a wingspan of over 2in (about 60mm): the male has a steely grey abdomen and eyes, a sharp contrast to the old gold colouration of the female. Look out, too, for the golden-ringed dragonfly, one of the largest British dragonflies, with its distinctive, wasp-like yellow and black rings, and the aptly-named small red damselfly, with its wing-span rarely exceeding 1¼in (35mm) and its bright red abdomen.

Valley bogs are also home to snipe and curlew. Walkers usually hear snipe before they see them, their alarm screech when flushed from cover being followed by a distinctive zig-zag flights. In the breeding season, snipe have an equally distinctive display flight, diving vertically from a great height while 'drumming' by vibrating their tail feathers. A complete contrast to the snipe's percussive call and drumming is the rippling call of the curlew, the most haunting of any of the moor's birds. Unfortunately, the numbers of breeding snipe and curlew are falling, possibly due to disturbance by people and dogs.

Above: Gallaven Mire

Below: The curlew is named for its bubbling call, one of the most haunting of any moorland bird. Its long curved beak is used to probe the moorland vegetation for insects (Mark Hamblin)

HEATH

On the fringes of the blanket bog, and on the drier eastern section of the moor is an area of heathland whose plant cover creates the picture postcard sea of purple heather in late summer. Heather is the predominant plant of the upland heath, often interspersed with clumps of western gorse (rather than the common gorse), whose bright yellow flowers add not only a contrast to the purple heather, but a surprising sweet, almondy smell on warm summer mornings. The upland heath also supports cross-leaved heath, purple moorgrass and bilberry, and is home to the red grouse. Red grouse is now considered by many experts to be a sub-species of the willow grouse, an Arctic bird. Red grouse occur only in the British Isles and Dartmoor is the southern limit of its range. The cackling alarm call of the grouse as it flees, fast and low, after being flushed is one of the most distinctive of any moorland bird. The upland heath is also home to the skylark and the ring ouzel. The number of skylarks in Britain has been falling for many years, giving rise to concern over its continuing status as one of the countryside's best-loved birds, its song evocative of lazy sunny days. On Dartmoor, skylarks are still relatively abundant, and it is hoped that the moor will play a part in the re-establishment of the bird elsewhere. Visitors to the megaliths of Drizzlecombe, to the south of Burrator Reservoir, will be interested to know that the local name for the valley was 'Thrushel Combe', meaning skylark valley. It is believed that early surveyors mistook the local Devonian pronunciation of 'thrushel' for 'drizzle', Dartmoor folk hardening the 'th' sound almost to a 'd' and making an 'izz' of 'ush'. To emphasise the old, proper name, skylarks can still be heard in their valley.

The ring ouzel, perhaps best described as a blackbird with a vicar's collar (though the male ring ouzel is actually chocolate brown rather than black) is more usually associated with northern moors, where its numbers have been declining over recent years. Again, therefore, the Dartmoor stock is of national importance.

Other birds associated with Dartmoor's upland heath include the handsome stonechat and the raven. One bird which the visitor may see in winter, but which is sadly no longer a Dartmoor breeding resident, is the merlin. The

David Jordan swaling on Gidleigh Common. The Common, like many others on Dartmoor, was recently entered into an ESA (Environmentally Sensitive Area) agreement which involved de-stocking to encourage the flora and fauna to flourish. However, the old system of swaling is still encouraged as part of the management of the moor

Below: A female common lizard basking in the sun
Bottom: Whinchat (both photographs Mark Hamblin)

last reliable breeding record is in 1967: the decline in heather coverage, particularly mature, tall heather, is believed to been responsible for the loss. Heather has been lost due to overgrazing of the upland heath and also by the over or accidental burning of areas of moorland. Properly done, controlled burning (or *swaling*) is a vital component of heather management. In both cases bracken has moved in to cover former heather-clad hillsides. The National Park Authority has introduced a code of practice covering burning, and it is hoped to halt the decline in heather. Whether the decline can be reversed and the merlin can once again be added to the checklist of Dartmoor birds remains to be seen.

On sunny days, the more open and drier sections of heath are used as basking sites for common lizards and adders. The latter are of little danger to the visitor, the footfalls of approaching walkers usually causing them to head quickly for cover.

Dartmoor's upland heath is the last British home of a particular form of hover fly, and another of the heath's rare insects is the emperor moth. These large, handsome moths, with their four striking wing 'eyes', develop from large emerald green caterpillars which feed on heather.

A distinction is usually made between upland and lowland heath, though the height at which the change over takes place is somewhat arbitrary, as the change in wildlife is dependent on the shelter from prevailing winds as well as altitude. On Dartmoor it is usually claimed that upland heath lies above 1,000ft (300m).

There is little change in vegetation, though the heather cover includes more bell heather among the ling than is usually fond on the upland heaths. As on the upland heathers, stonechats are a characteristic bird, and where the lowland heath is forested at its edge, tree pipits can be seen. On the eastern edge of the moor a major addition to Dartmoor's checklist of birds was the arrival of the Dartford warbler in the early 1990s. The warbler had until very recently been confined to the remnant heathland of Dorset, but a succession of mild winters has allowed it to extend its range. On eastern Dartmoor there are also breeding pairs of nightjars, another bird whose numbers are giving cause for concern. The nightjar flies at dusk and is rarely seen by the casual visitor, though its call – a little like a sewing machine – can occasionally be heard.

Unfortunately, the arrival of the Dartford warbler has been countered by the loss of the silver-studded blue butterfly. The blue was a small and easily missed butterfly, but its loss is significant as it has declined rapidly throughout its British range.

THE MOORLAND FRINGE

Large tracts of grass moorland, particularly at the edge of the moor proper, are to be found on Dartmoor, the principal grasses being sheep's fescue, common and bristle bent. Here patches of tormentil and heath milkwort occur. In more sheltered spots, particularly where bracken excludes grazing animals, the pale lilac heath dog violet and the daisy-like lawn camomile can be found. Each of these species is declining nationally, Dartmoor being an important conservation area for both.

Though a much poorer habitat than heath, the grass moor does support large populations of both whinchats and wheatears, as well as skylarks and meadow larks. It is also an important butterfly habitat. Ironically, as it finds few friends among conservationists, the bracken which has invaded the overgrazed grass moors is home to the high brown and pearl-bordered fritillaries. The larger high brown is found in only three areas of Britain, again making the Dartmoor population of national importance.

Areas of purple moorgrass and rushes, too dry to be classed as valley bogs but too wet to support heathland vegetation, are classified as *rhos* pasture, from the Welsh word for such damp areas of the moorland fringe. On Dartmoor, the main rush of the pastures is sharp-flowered rush which grows up to 3ft (1m) tall and has brownish-green flowers. Among the grass and rushes grow the beautiful meadow thistle, ivy-leaved bellflower with its lilac trumpet-like flowers, the pink-flowered heath spotted orchid, and devil's-bit scabious, its deep purple flower heads almost as distinctive as the red-purple thistles. The pastures are also the southern limit of the cranberry, a low creeping evergreen shrub with distinctive red, pear-shaped berries.

The pasture's flowers support good colonies of marbled white and small pearl-bordered butterflies, and is one of Europe's most important sites for the marsh fritillary. The pastures are also a nationally-important site for the narrow-bordered bee hawk moth, a day-flying moth which is nowhere near as large as its name. The moth has almost transparent wings and resembles a bumble bee in flight. Its caterpillars feed on devil's-bit scabious. The Dartmoor pastures are also one of the last British strongholds of the southern damselfly. The males of this delicate species are pale blue and black, the females dark green and black.

The pastures support breeding colonies of snipe, reed buntings and grasshopper warblers and overwintering flocks of woodcock. Descending from the high moor, they are also the first Dartmoor habitat to support resident groups of large mammals. Although foxes can be found on the upland moors, the harsh winter climate and poor feeding potential discourages permanent residence. In the pastures however, there are roe deer and dormice appear in the woodland fringe.

As well as *rhos* (wet) pastures, the moorland fringe has dry pastures, some of which have been converted into hay meadows. The flowers of such areas include those of *rhos* pastures (heath spotted orchid, devil's-bit scabious) and grass moorland (heath violet, western gorse) but also a number of different species, ox-eye daisy, the violet-flowered self-heal, the densely red-flower-headed great burnet, which grows in large patches, and heath bedstraw.

The dry pastures of the eastern moorland fringe also support several rarities, such as a rare form of eyebright long thought extinct in south-west England, which was rediscovered in 1995, while the scarce Deptford pink, a delicate bright pink flower, grows near Buckfastleigh. The greater butterfly orchid, which has green-tinged white flowers, is abundant in certain Dartmoor locations, but is now scarce in other parts of Britain.

Of bird life, the moor's dry pastures are most notable for the cirl bunting, a bird now found almost nowhere else in Britain. This striking bird is similar to the yellowhammer, but the male has a distinct black collar and eye stripe, and it feeds on the grasshoppers which thrive in the pastures.

WOODLAND

Although most of the National Park's woodland lies in the lower valleys, there are wooded areas even on the upland moor, though grazing has reduced the former cover to a handful of sites. Of the upland woods, special mention must be made of Wistman's Wood, Black Tor Copse and Piles Copse, which are thought to be

THE LARGE BLUE BUTTERFLY

Sadly, one of the rarest of Dartmoor's wildlife species, the large blue butterfly, became extinct in 1979. At that time the Dartmoor breeding site of the butterfly was the last known site in Britain. The large blue has one of the most extraordinary life cycles of any insect. Its caterpillars feed on thyme, but when full grown drop to the ground where they secrete a liquid which ants find irresistible. The ants take the caterpillar back to their nest where it feeds on ant grubs while being 'milked'. It hibernates in the nest, then becomes a chrysalis and the emergent adult crawls out of the ant nest before spreading its wings. The butterfly is declining throughout Europe and, fearing total extinction, Swedish stock have now been reintroduced to the moor.

Late spring on Dartmoor, with bluebells, gorse and mountain ash

remnant sections of original moor oak woodland preserved by the clitter on which they grow and which has successfully defended them from grazing. The three woods are important conservation areas, Wistman's Wood and Black Tor Copse are National Nature Reserves, but they are also magical places. Wistman's is especially evocative, its oaks stunted and wind-distorted. On misty mornings, the wood is one of the most romantic places on Dartmoor. But as well as being scenically attractive, the woods are of national importance for the mosses, lichens and liverworts which grow on, and beneath, the trees. These plants, particularly the lichens and more delicate mosses, are vulnerable to any increase in air-borne pollution levels, and the loss of a particular form of moss from Wistman's Wood where it was formerly abundant is, perhaps, an indicator that air quality is declining.

Although the three upland remnant oak woods are a spectacular Dartmoor survival, they are not the only examples of upland oakwoods in the National Park. Elsewhere there are nearly 5,000 acres (2,000ha) of natural or semi-natural woodland growing above the 820ft (250m) contour, although in these alder and ash usually supplement the pedunculate and sessile oaks, together with some beech, birch, rowan, hazel and holly. In particular areas there are lime and more unusual species such as the wild service tree. Of these lower – but still upland – oakwoods the most notable is Whiddon Deer Park near Castle Drogo, which is at least medieval in origin. This wood is of national importance for two specific mosses.

Elsewhere, Dartmoor's oakwoods are of importance for their lichens and mosses, some of which are extremely rare. One lichen grows at only two Dartmoor sites and one on Bodmin Moor, while another form is known only at Wistman's Wood and Black Tor Copse. Though many of the lichens are difficult to spot, one species is much easier, hanging in bunches from tree branches. This prominence is reflected in the lichen being one of the few to have an English name – it is the string-of-sausages lichen.

In the upland oak woods, the woodland floor is often carpeted with bluebells in spring, a memorable sight, while several – and most particular the Teign Valley woods – have wonderful springtime displays of wild daffodils. The woodland floor can also be covered with dog's mercury, with its greenish flowers, or ramsons, with its distinctive white lily flower and even more distinctive smell of garlic. The woodland species of flowers attract specific forms of butterfly, including the purple emperor, one of Britain's most magnificent butterflies, purple hairstreak and silver-washed fritillary, as well as more common species. In the 1950s the rare and beautiful white admiral butterfly colonised Dartmoor and is still a resident species. The woods are also an important habitat for other insects, most notably the blue ground beetle, which is known only at its Dartmoor sites, and a very rare type of rove beetle which lives in the nests of hornets.

The birds of the oak woods include tree pipits, great-spotted woodpeckers, redstarts and the pied flycatcher, which colonised Dartmoor in the 1950s.

At the edge of the wet pastures there are sometimes sections of wet woodland where the damp or waterlogged ground supports willow (both grey and goat), alder, downy birch and ash, rather than the more varied species of the oakwoods. Such woods are excellent for both wetland flowers and ferns. Of the flowers, marsh marigold with its large yellow flowers, marsh violet and the easily overlooked opposite-leaved golden saxifrage are most often found. The ferns include several unusual species – scaly male and broad buckler – as well as the more common, including the graceful lady fern. Perhaps the most sought after is the royal fern, one of Europe's tallest ferns. The birds of the wetland woods include redpoll, siskin and the now uncommon willow tit.

Much rarer birds inhabit Dartmoor's plantations of alien conifers. Crossbills breed in several and the goshawk arrived in the National Park during the 1980s. Though both species are an exciting addition to the Dartmoor checklist, and the conifers also attract goldcrests and siskins, it is hoped that no further acres of moorland will become plantations.

OTHER HABITATS

In addition to the major habitats considered above, there are a host of smaller habitats, all equally important to Dartmoor's wildlife. The tors and clitter and the old moorland quarries are home to more than sixty species of lichen, including several more commonly encountered in the Arctic, and some rare species found nowhere else in the country. In 1990, one species was found on Dartmoor for the first time in Britain. The outcrops also support several scarce species of fern. Forked spleenwort, its narrow fronds ending in a snake's tongue-like fork, is at the southern limit of its British range, while lanceolate spleenwort is at the northern limit of its European range. Equally rare is the flax-leaved St John's wort,

Overleaf: Looking towards Jurston Farm and Shapley Common in spring

Wildflowers in a Dartmoor lane

a rare flower with delicate yellow flowers, often red on the underside.

The farmland at the fringes of the moor supports song thrushes, skylarks, woodlarks, whitethroats, yellowhammers and cirl buntings and, as with the upland fringes, is patrolled by buzzards. The stone walls and hedges that separate the fields are also havens for wildlife. Dormice thrive here, as does the rare brown hairstreak butterfly.

The caves of the limestone outcrop near Buckfastleigh are home to one-third of Britain's population of greater horseshoe bats, as well as a rare form of blind shrimp.

Equally important are Dartmoor's streams and reservoirs. The old dialect word for a river was *ta*, explaining the names Taw, Teign and Tavy, and also Henry Williamson's choice of *Tarka* for the otter in his most famous book. It is appropriate therefore that the otter has re-established itself in most of Dartmoor's rivers. In contrast, the salmon has declined, possibly due to oceanic over-fishing, although changes to spawning grounds cannot be ruled out. The rivers support populations of kingfisher, dipper and grey wagtail, and goosanders breed on the Dart. The rivers and reservoirs are also important sites for dragonflies and damselflies, with several nationally scarce species being well represented. Of the former, the common and southern hawkers are the most spectacular, while the beautiful damselfly lives up to its name, the male with purple wings and a blue body, the female having a green body and almost transparent wings.

HABITAT MANAGEMENT

The unique quality of Dartmoor is its remarkable assemblage of habitats and species, and it is the aim of the National Park Authority and other conservation bodies to not only maintain the present wildlife habitats, but to restore, as far as possible, such deterioration as has occurred. To this end, recolonisation of extinct species is being encouraged and reintroduction will be considered where such re-establishment is not possible.

To ensure the survival of existing, recolonising and new species the moor's habitats are being positively managed. On the northern moor, military activity involving heavy munitions has ceased and a reduction in overall activity is being sought. Efforts are also being made to restore the blanket bog coverage. Further loss of upland heath to grass and bracken will be prevented, and the spread of heather will be encouraged. As noted above, the National Park Authority in partnership has already prepared a code of practice covering swaling (burning) of moorland, and has issued a code of conduct on letterboxing which, in certain sensitive areas, threatens lichens and breeding birds. Many native woodlands are being actively managed. A felling policy which maximises the wildlife potential and landscape benefits of conifer plantations is being sought, and individual programmes aimed at conserving rare species are also being undertaken.

The aim of these conservation efforts is to maintain Dartmoor's pre-eminence as a landscape combining wild, natural and cultural elements.

Wild broom in full flower, Mardon Down

DARTMOOR PONIES

High Dartmoor is a harsh place for animals, and
visitors would be very lucky to see truly wild animals.
What they will almost certainly see are Dartmoor
ponies. So much a part of the moorland scene are
these hardy ponies that when Dartmoor was made a
National Park in 1951, a pony was chosen as the
National Park's symbol.

The history of the Dartmoor pony is a long one,
hoof prints having been found within a Bronze Age
settlement on Shaugh Moor, suggesting that 4,000
years ago the pony – or its ancestor – was already a
working animal. From that time until the internal
combustion engine became cheap enough to replace
them, ponies were the beasts of burden on the moor.
They carried the farmers around their land, hauled
carts of farm produce to market, and, as pack
animals, carried Dartmoor's mineral and wool wealth
off the moor. In the last years of the nineteenth
century there was a sharp increase in the number of
pit ponies required by the coal mines of South Wales
and Somerset, and the Dartmoor ponies, small but
very strong and hardy, were ideal for the purpose. But
with the decline in moorland industries and the
mechanisation of the distant coal mines, there was
less need for the animals and numbers fell. Over
recent years there has been a dramatic reduction in
numbers, from around 30,000 at the end of the
1939-45 war to about 3,000 today: not only are
ponies no longer required as working animals, but
there is less call for horse meat and no European
Union subsidies for pony rearing.

Most ponies are now sold as children's ponies,
either directly or through riding schools. This has led
to the ponies being crossed with more 'attractive'
breeds. As a result, although some pure stock
remains, many of the moor's ponies are cross-bred
and are less able to withstand the rigours of the
Dartmoor winter.

The ponies are not truly wild: they all have
owners, and carry distinctive ear or tail marks, or
brands. But they are unbroken, coming into contact
with their owners only at the pony 'drifts' (round-ups)
each autumn, so it is advisable not to get too close as
they may bite or kick. And please remember that it is
against the law to feed them as it encourages them
to stay close to the road. Tragically, each year many
ponies are killed or injured by traffic.

3 Man's influence

Above: An aerial view of Grimspound, with Haytor in the distance

Opposite: Grey Wethers double stone circle

As the ice sheets that covered the land to the north of Dartmoor shrank and the moorland permafrost melted, trees colonised the area. It is likely that Man moved in soon after, flint tools dating from the Mesolithic (Middle Stone) Age having been found which probably date from as early as 8,000BC. From that time Man's occupation of Dartmoor has been continuous, though it was to take several thousand years before a permanent reminder of that presence was left on the landscape.

Neolithic people buried their dead in tombs made of large slabs of stone, usually three or four uprights capped with another flat slab. The tomb was then earthed over to form a long barrow. Over time, and particularly on exposed sites, the earth mound sometimes eroded or blew away, leaving the tomb slabs open to the elements. Such a tomb is known as a cromlech or dolmen, and one of the best in Devon lies within the National Park. It is known as Spinster's Rock and lies to the west of Drewsteignton. It takes the standard form, with three upright slabs and a thick capping slab, and its name reflects the awe in which such sites were held by cultures remote in time from the Neolithic builders.

All over Britain cromlechs have been woven into local folklore, usually seen as the work of the Devil, giants or mythical heroes. Here the name dates from

THE MEGALITHS OF DARTMOOR

Although it has nothing to compare in size with Stonehenge or Avebury, Dartmoor has one of the highest concentrations of megalithic sites in Britain, and also some of the most interesting. Megalith (from the Greek mega lithos, large stone) is used as a blanket term covering stone circles, rows and single standing stones, all of which are represented on the moor.

It is usually assumed that the stones were erected by early Bronze Age peoples, though as Neolithic folk were skilled at raising such stones – as their long barrows testify – it is possible that there was a continuity of the practice across the arbitrary delineation of the two ages.

The simplest form of megalith is the single stone or menhir (from the Welsh, ie Celtic, maen hir, long stone). There are many of these on the moor, though care must be taken in identifying them as later folk also erected or modified standing stones as memorials, or to mark cross-moor routes. Of the prehistoric stones, the finest are in Drizzlecombe, south of Burrator Reservoir. One of these, at over 13ft (4m) is the tallest on Dartmoor.

The Drizzlecombe menhir is associated with a whole complex of sites, the valley having three stone rows and several burial cairns, including the vast Giant's Basin, which is 82ft (25m) in diameter and over 6ft (2m) high. The Drizzlecombe rows are relatively short and, in part, of single stones. Much more complex are the Merrivale rows, two of which are of double stones. These two double rows are not parallel, but are aligned with the May rise of Pleiades, a group of stars the Greeks are said to have used to predict the time of harvesting. With the increased credence given to the theory that Stonehenge and other stone circles were astronomical calendars, this alignment is intriguing.

The Merrivale stone rows are among the easiest for

visitors to see as they lie close to a road. More dedication is needed to see the far more imposing row that starts on Erme Plains, on the southern moor, and ends on Green Hill. The row is of double stones and, at nearly 2 miles (3km) is perhaps the longest in the world, much longer than the famous rows at Carnac in Brittany, though its stones are much smaller. The row is also intriguing for not being straight, and for each end not being visible from the other, and it also crosses a river.

At its southern end, the Erme row starts from a stone circle, the most well-known type of megalithic site. There are several good circles on Dartmoor including an undisturbed one on Scorhill, although many others have been considerably restored so that their original form has been lost (making the possibility of discovering any critical sunrise or sunset alignments almost impossible).

To the east of Sittaford Tor, the Grey Wethers circle is named for the similarity of the stones to sheep (wethers in the local dialect) when viewed from a distance. Legend has it that the 'flock' was once sold by a local to a gullible newcomer.

Although new discoveries are being made, it is likely that we will never know the exact reason for the construction of the megalithic sites, other than the simplistic view that some form of ritual, probably associated with death and possibly with the sun or stars, took place at them. But our relative ignorance merely adds to the enigmatic beauty of the sites. Whether the visitor tends towards the 'earth magic' view of the stones (as reservoirs of spiritual energy and so on), or to the more scientific view, there is no doubting that the stones have a wonderful presence.

Below left: Merrivale stone row

Below: Beardown Man, prehistoric standing stone

Round Pound, the most massively walled of Dartmoor's pounds, is also one of its most enigmatic. It seems too small to have been an animal compound, though some experts suggest its internal walls are not original, perhaps added later by a shepherd or by local tinners. Evidence of iron smelting has been found on the site, and it has even been suggested that it may have been the workshop of an Iron Age blacksmith

Opposite: Taken from Combestone Tor, this photograph shows a parallel reave system above the River Dart. The finding of reaves by examining aerial photographs of the moor has required a major reassessment of early farming practices on Dartmoor

medieval times when the wool trade was a cottage industry. Three sisters who were spinsters (the name given to women who operated spinning wheels, though the sisters may also have been spinsters in the modern sense) are said to have erected the stones when they had a few minutes to spare while on their way to their buyer.

In medieval times, it was often believed that such tombs covered buried treasure, and digging often caused the rock slabs to fall. It is known that Spinsters' Rock has been reconstructed, although it is thought that the present form is a reasonable representation of the original, and, for a people with few mechanical aids, it represents an impressive piece of engineering.

Dartmoor's long barrows lie on prominent sites, but below the level where, it is believed, much of the country was largely forested. Many of the tomb sites must therefore have been cleared of trees, as must the surrounding area so that the site's prominence could be appreciated. Pollen analysis suggests the trees were cleared by burning. It is assumed that this was for early forms of agriculture, but there is little hard evidence to support this – there is, for instance, no evidence of permanent dwellings. Were the Neolithic folk still a nomadic people who cleared areas of trees to encourage forest animals into the open for ease of hunting, or for their own herds, returning to the tombs they built only at certain ritual times?

Whatever the actual life style of Dartmoor's early Neolithic people, it is clear that by the time metal working folk arrived on the moorland, the tree cover had been largely cleared and permanent sites were being occupied. The coming of the first metal workers is usually said to be the start of the Bronze Age, though in reality it is likely that copper was the first metal to have been smelted. Alloying the copper with tin – of which there is plenty on Dartmoor (though little evidence to suggest is was extracted in prehistoric times) – made bronze, a harder metal than copper, allowing the crafting of tools and weapons which could take and maintain a sharper edge.

Dartmoor has the largest and one of the most important concentrations of Bronze Age remains in Britain, and while it is obviously true that the relative poverty of the moor from an agricultural point of view in later ages contributed to the survival of many sites – which in more fertile areas might have been ploughed into oblivion – it is clear that the moor was a valuable asset. All over the moor there are hut circles (at least 1,500 have been recorded to date), which are the bases of Bronze Age huts. A circular wall of stones, whose collection would have also helped to clear the moor of boulders inconvenient to herding or planting, was topped by branches which leaned inwards on to a central, vertical pole. A conical roof was then created by laying animal skins or turf over the branches. Many of the huts were floored with stone slabs, as earth floors rapidly turn to mud in wet weather. The huts vary in size from 10ft (3m) to about 32ft (10m) in diameter, the wall being about 3ft (1m) high, and having a doorway formed by two upright stone portals. Although in may cases the walls are now much lower, the huts having formed a convenient quarry for later wall-building farmers, at most sites the lowest ring of stones and the doorways are still visible. Sometimes the huts occur singularly, or in small groups, suggesting use by herders or families, but occasionally they are in numbers which imply 'village' settlements.

At Grimspound, on Hamel Down to the north-west of Widecombe-in-the-Moor, a circular wall almost 10ft (3m) thick and known to have been about 6ft (2m) tall in the eighteenth century (and perhaps even to have been a double wall) encloses an area of about 4 acres (1.6ha) in which stand the remains of some two dozen hut circles. The position of this settlement makes it clear it was not defensive (against attacks by people that is), and the enclosed area seems too small to have been for cultivation. It is conjectured that it was used for stock, perhaps during the lambing or calving season when the young animals would have been easier prey for the wolves which still roamed England. It is likely that other, smaller pounds, such as that in the Erme valley on the southern moor, and Round Pound near Shovel Down, were also for animals. Round Pound has a central hut circle and is sub-divided, and may have been used by a shepherd.

Bronze Age folk buried their dead in stone chambers too, but rather than the elaborate, above ground, tombs of the Neolithic period, these chambers were smaller – boxes would be a better description – and placed just below the ground. The boxes were of flat stones, the 'lid' lying at ground level. Inside larger boxes the body would be crouched, but more usually cremated remains were placed in

THE REAVE SYSTEM

It is interesting to note that the idea of the pounds being for animals has not always been accepted, and even now there are occasional dissenting voices who see the enclosed areas as cultivated land, the walls being to keep domestic and wild animals away from valuable crops. In the days before the discovery of Dartmoor's reave system this suggestion could not be lightly dismissed, but the reaves seem to finally disprove it. Reaves were only discovered – or at least their full extent and complexity was only realised – when aerial photography of the moor was undertaken. Reaves are banks of earth or stone running parallel across the moor, sometimes for many miles, and invariably ending at a reave running at right-angles to the rows. It is assumed that the reaves were ancient field systems, the banks separating land allocated to individuals or communities and also keeping stock off the crops.

Kistvaen, Drizzlecombe

much smaller boxes. The boxes – called *kistvaens* or *cists* – are usually covered with cairns of stones, some, as at Drizzlecombe, forming very large heaps. Other cists have been found at the centre of stone circles.

Although the reave systems and the hut circles imply a fixed population, it is possible that Bronze Age people were involved in transhumance, the twice-annual migration which is still practised in parts of southern Europe. Animals are moved on to higher ground during the summer months, then back to the sheltered valleys when winter arrives. Perhaps Dartmoor's people occupied the moor for the growing season, then retreated south to the coast to fish during the winter.

CELTS AND SAXONS

Around 1000BC, the climate of Dartmoor declined and this, together with the increased coverage of blanket bog, made the moor less attractive for both crops and grazing. The moor seems to have been deserted by about 500BC, though the moorland fringe, particularly on the eastern side, shows evidence of the next great cultural wave sweeping in from mainland Europe – the iron-using Celts.

In Britain it seems that the Celts absorbed rather than replaced the Bronze Age inhabitants, though it is clear that the newcomers were a more tribal and warlike people. The Celtic tribes built 'hillforts' into which they could retreat when threatened, choosing hill tops which they reinforced with ditches and ramparts. In the Teign valley, to the north of Moretonhampstead, Cranbrook Castle and Prestonbury Castle are two such hillforts, the best examples in the National

Clapper bridge across the Wallabrook

Park. Some experts have suggested that these two forts protected the Teign valley, the river being an easily utilised route into the area, but that may be to read into the hillforts much more significance than their builders intended.

Beyond the deserted moor, the Celts were eventually absorbed into the Roman empire. *Isca Dumnuniorum*, or Exeter as we now call it, was the administrative capital of the Roman south-west. But the Celts soon re-established their tribal way of life when the legionaries went home to confront the barbarians on Rome's doorstep. Legend has it that these tribal conflicts led one Celtic leader to import Saxon mercenaries from northern Europe and then to discover, to his and England's cost, that the problem with mercenary armies is that they can be difficult to send home. The Saxons settled in Kent and then pushed west. Their progress was halted, probably by the real King Arthur, in the early sixth century, but they were patient invaders and after a generation or so of waiting, they picked up their swords and shields and headed west again. In 577, at Dyrham near Bristol, they divided the western Celts in two, pushing them into Wales and along the south-west peninsula to Dartmoor and the border of Cornwall. To the Saxons the Celts were *wallas*, foreigners, a name derived from the Velcae tribe the Saxons had fought on the mainland. The name is the root of Wales, of Walloon in Belgium, Valais in Switzerland, Vlachs in Romania and of Dartmoor's Wallabrook, because when the Saxons reached the river they found Celts living there.

With the arrival of the Saxons, the settlement of Dartmoor and the moorland fringes was established much as it is now, though for the Wessex kings who ruled the area, establishing a kingdom was much easier than maintaining it. In the last years of the eighth century, Offa built his dyke to separate the Saxons and the Celts of Wales, but no such boundary existed between the Devon Saxons and the Cornish Celts. That left the western edge of Wessex vulnerable, and during the Viking raids of the first half of the ninth century, longboats manoeuvred up the Tamar so that an attack could be launched eastwards. The attack forced King Alfred to retreat into deepest Somerset from where, having regrouped, he emerged to rout the Norsemen. To defend Wessex from a renewed attack from the west, Alfred built a series of *burhs*, or fortresses. Those at Exeter, Barnstaple and Totnes protected the rivers into Devon, while that at Lydford, at the north-western corner of the National Park, defended the approach via the Tamar. The

Below: Lydford Castle is not a true castle – the remains of a Norman castle lie close to the river – but a gaol for offenders against the moor's forest and stannary laws

Lydford site became so important that a settlement grew up, its streets laid out on a grid pattern that the present village still follows, and a royal mint was opened. The mint struck Lydford pennies from locally mined silver, some of which can be seen in the Royal Museum in Stockholm having formed part of *Danegeld*, the bribe paid to the Vikings to stay away from Wessex. But despite the Lydford fortress, Viking raids continued, and in 997, longboats sailed up the Tamar and both Lydford and Tavistock were sacked and burned.

THE MEDIEVAL MOOR

Lydford church is dedicated to St Petroc, an early Celtic saint, implying that the Saxons of Devon were converting from the old religion as a result of contact with the Christian Celts. There are two more churches dedicated to the saint on the edge of the southern moor.

Opposite: (top) Higher Shilstone farm is a typical Dartmoor longhouse where humans and animals shared the same building. Originally a medieval open hall, with a central cross passage, the building underwent considerable architectural enhancement with mullioned windows and beautifully carved doorways. The arched doorway next to the steps reflects this period when a new separate entrance was made into the shippon; (below) Hound Tor medieval village. The village of Hundatora can trace its origins to Saxon times. The village was abandoned at the time of the Black Death in the fourteenth century

Lydford church was important to the new Dartmoor folk as it had the only consecrated ground close to the northern moor, bodies being carried across the moor for burial along a route which can still be followed. The way was, and is, called the Lich Way, *lich* being an ancient word for a corpse which lives on in lich gate, the entrance gate to a churchyard where the coffin was placed so the bearers could get their breath before the last carry into the church.

The moorland dwellers whose remains were transported along the Lich Way lived in houses quite different from those of their Bronze Age predecessors. Their longhouses were, as the name implies, long buildings, relatively narrow and roofed with thatch over wooden beams. The family lived at one end in a slightly raised section, while the other, lower end was occupied by their animals. The cooking fire stood on a stone plinth beneath a hole in the roof and a central drain – no more than a narrow channel cut in the floor – carried away animal waste. The arrangement must have been cold, draughty, smoky, smelly and would fail any modern hygiene standard, but some longhouses (though of late, rather than early, medieval vintage) still survive – most notably at Shilstone, near Throwleigh, close to the northern edge of the moor – suggesting, yet again, that modern standards are very modern indeed.

Longhouses were occasionally grouped together in settlements, many of the settlements having evolved into today's moorland villages. However, some were abandoned and a study of these – most notably the fine remains between Hound

Tor and Greator Rocks, near Manaton and Widecombe-in-the-Moor – suggests that moorland living in the medieval period was not easy. There were three long-houses and eight outbuildings, three of the latter having kilns which imply that harvested grain needed to be dried before long-term storage. Clearly Dartmoor's climate was wet. The land was also hard to work, although the Hound Tor site was on the moor's relatively fertile eastern slopes.

After the Norman conquest, upland Dartmoor was a royal hunting 'forest', with ditches – which allowed deer into the forest but prevented them from leaving it – separating the upland from the moorland fringe, where farmers worked an open field system. Each farmer would be given strips of land in the field, the strips being changed annually so good and bad land was shared evenly. But the moor often had more poor land than good, and the strip system was an inefficient way of farming.

Some experts claim that Hound Tor village was deserted when the farming became uneconomic, forcing the villagers to move into the valleys. Others claim that Black Death is likely to have killed all the inhabitants of such places, the way of life – with everyone in such close proximity – meaning that the disease spread quickly and with lethal efficiency. When the plague finally abated, there were too few people left, and the living at Hound Tor was too hard for the village to be re-occupied. It is also possible that the landowners, the great abbeys at the edge of the moor, cleared the tenants to maximise the land that could be used for sheep grazing. This sounds an outrageous claim, but in other places in England the monastic houses are known to have carried out such clearances.

Although Tavistock and Buckfast Abbeys were originally founded for Benedictine monks in Saxon times, it was during the Norman period, the 'great age' of English monasticism, that they flourished. Buckfast was refounded for Cistercian monks in 1147. The Cistercian way of life was a punishing schedule of work and prayer, the work including the creation of the wool industry which made England an economic giant in medieval Europe. The best wool came from Cotswold sheep, but even the poorer quality fleeces from Dartmoor sheep were valuable. The monks of Buckfast Abbey especially worked to introduce sheep rearing on the poorer moor soils

Top: Siward's Cross, with Nun's Cross farm behind. Siward's Cross marks the outer boundary of the monastic lands of Buckland Abbey. It is one of many crosses that waymarked the monks' path between Buckfast, Tavistock and Buckland; (above) one of the T/A waymarking stones at Merrivale

and cereal production of the more fertile areas. The size of the grange barn near the present abbey's ancient north gate is a tribute to their success in the latter, while the wealth of the most of England's monasteries indicates their success with wool production.

Ultimately, of course, it was the power and wealth of the monasteries that led Henry VIII – frightened of the first and greedy for the second – to dissolve them. But by then the changes the abbeys had introduced to English farming were complete; changes which could not be undone and still form the basis of today's farming system. They were also the reason for the growth of Dartmoor's towns and villages. Lydford, the Saxon fortress town, was soon overtaken in importance by Tavistock and Buckfastleigh which grew up around their abbeys, and by the

market towns which grew up on the moorland fringe – Ashburton, Bovey Tracey, Chagford, Moretonhampstead and Okehampton. On the routes between those major towns smaller villages grew out of early settlements – Widecombe-in-the-Moor, Holne and Peter Tavy. Of the Dartmoor settlements, only Princetown has origins later than the medieval period.

The abbeys may also have been responsible for creating tracks across Dartmoor, and a glance at maps of the moor reveals the existence of several paths marked as 'Abbot's Way'. It is thought that these linked the abbeys, and the abbeys to the trading centres where their wool and farm produce could be sold. In reality, tracks across the moor had existed from prehistoric times, but it is likely that the abbeys erected waymarkers – some, at least, of the crosses that can be found even in the most remote areas of the moor – and also built some of the moor's famous clapper bridges.

Of the crosses, perhaps the most famous is Siward's Cross, to the east of Burrator Reservoir, which is known to have stood there since 1240, when a record of the lands of Buckfast Abbey notes it as marking an eastern border. The cross's name may derive from the Northumbrian Earl Siward who held lands in Devon in the eleventh century or, more prosaically, a local, thirteenth-century family. The alternative name of Nun's Cross which is sometimes seen almost certainly has nothing to do with nuns, probably deriving from *nant*, the Celtic name for a stream. Other crosses are placed at the top of climbs up the moorland edge. These were known as 'Thank God' crosses, allowing the weary traveller, struggling breathlessly up the slope, to stop for a rest knowing the climb was over, and to thank God it was.

Several centuries after the monks had raised their crosses, an Act of Parliament in 1696 required towns at the moorland edge to place waymarkers along routes between them to aid travellers in bad weather. These, too, can still be seen. A number of waymarkers pass close to the standing stones at Merrivale, which pre-date it by over 5,000 years, and are marked 'T/A' for Tavistock/Ashburton.

DARTMOOR CLAPPERS

In 1968, the Post Office issued a set of commemorative stamps. The letter post (four old penny) stamp bore the image of Tarr Steps, a famous clapper bridge on Exmoor, beneath which it said 'Prehistoric'. This attribution has coloured many views on the age of the Dartmoor clappers, and while it is possibly – perhaps even probable – that ancient Man used handy granite slabs to bridge streams, it is now believed that all the existing clapper bridges date from medieval times (if the fact that many have been rebuilt several times after being demolished by flood waters is ignored).

To see the development of river crossing technology on Dartmoor, go to Dartmeet. There, stepping stones – surely the first form of river crossing – cross the West Dart River, while a fine clapper and a more modern (but still old) bridge crosses the East Dart River.

The clapper is the simplest form of bridge, a flat slab placed on pillars of stones set in the stream bed. Occasionally, as at Postbridge, the pillars are tall and fashioned on their upstream side so as to deflect the water – designed to allow the bridge to remain intact and serviceable when the river rose. The bridge slabs were wide so that packhorses could use them easily. The packhorses would have carried the abbot's wool and they would also have carried tin, the metal whose exploitation was the basis of the Dartmoor economy for centuries and has left a scattering of romantic ruins across the high moor.

DARTMOOR'S TIN INDUSTRY

Although the Romans mined tin in Cornwall they do not seem to have worked the cassiterite (tin ore) deposits of Dartmoor. As there is no evidence of Bronze Age working, it is therefore assumed that the moor's tin industry started only in the twelfth century. It is likely that the ore was first discovered in streams which had cut down through the cassiterite deposits (lodes), and that water was the first extraction method used by the early miners. Streams were diverted and dammed, the breaking of the dam causing a rush of water that would tear away the topsoil and expose the lode. Streaming, as the process was called, was very destructive of the landscape, its scars still being evident in places on the moor. The ore was processed on the moor, crude furnaces producing an impure metal which was pack-horsed to Ashburton, Chagford, Plympton or Tavistock. These were Dartmoor's 'stannary' towns – named from *stannum*, Latin for tin (the chemical symbol for tin is still Sn) – where the manufactured tin was taxed. In the early days, tin was alloyed with lead to produce pewter. With the decline in the use of pewter for plates and mugs, the Dartmoor tin industry declined too, but was boosted again when tin was needed for solders and plate.

Streaming was not only a destructive but a relatively inefficient way of obtaining ore. Open-cast mining or the use of horizontal adits (tunnels) replaced it, these being supplemented by shaft mining as soon as the problems of pumping water from vertical shafts had been overcome. To reduce transport costs a purer form of tin was required and this required hotter furnaces. Water wheels were therefore constructed, and leats were dug to provide the water to turn them. The wheels powered bellows which pumped air to the furnaces, raising their temperature. The ruins of the blowing houses, as these bellows-driven furnace buildings were called, are a feature of many of Dartmoor's tin mine ruins. The waterwheels also powered crushing mills where the mined rock was stamped between hammers and granite mortar stones.

The crushed rock was passed through settling pits (buddles) from where the tin ore could be removed, reducing the flow of waste through the furnace. After smelting, the liquid tin was poured into a granite mould stone to create an almost pure ingot ready for transport. Mould stones and stones bearing the imprint of the ore stamps can also be found at mine ruins. Other interesting relics which can be found at mine sites include tinners' huts, where tinners stayed or sheltered at remote mine sites, and caches where tools and equipment were stored when the miners went home for the weekend. Of the latter the most famous are Downing's House by the River Erme and the Beehive Hut to the north of Postbridge. In each case there are legends of the huts housing illicit stills and even contraband, brought north from the coast.

Another ruin often associated with the tin mining industry is the rabbit warren, varying in size from the small-scale 'pillow mounds', which can be seen in several moorland valleys, to major warren systems covering many acres as, for instance, at Ditsworthy Warren to the south-east of Burrator Reservoir. In each case the rabbits were encouraged to settle and breed, then trapped to feed the miners. At Ditsworthy, the job of warrener was full-time and a house was provided for his use.

Curiously, despite the fact that they ate them, the miners had a high regard for the rabbit which, like themselves, worked the harsh moor and tunnelled into the earth. Consequently the miners took the rabbit as their symbol, though the actual form it took – three rabbits each with only one ear – is believed by some to be an allusion to the Holy Trinity. The symbol can be seen on a carved boss in several

Opposite top: Headland Warren farm, where there is considerable evidence of tin mining. It is said that a mid-nineteenth century landlord of the Warren House Inn used to display a sign to attract the miners:

Jan Roberts lives here,
Sells cider and beer
Your hearts to cheer.
And if you want meat
To make up a treat
Here be rabbits to eat.

Opposite below: Pillow mounds, Ditsworthy. Pillow mounds were early forms of rabbit warrens, created to provide a home for rabbits which could then be farmed for their meat to enhance the miners' otherwise meagre diet

Top: Tinner's mould stone, River Walkham
Above: Medieval boss depicting the tinners' rabbits, church of St Mary the Virgin, Throwleigh

moorland churches. Ultimately Dartmoor's rabbits became a pest. Myxamatosis was deliberately introduced in 1954 to reduce numbers and two years later warrening was officially ended.

In medieval times, the tin miners of Dartmoor were a national asset, and were given exemption from ordinary laws, a fact which doubtless attracted some men to what was a hard, lonely and sometimes dangerous profession. The miners were subject only to stannary law which was administered by the Stannary Courts at the four stannary towns. Stannary law was enacted by a Stannary Parliament which usually met at Crockern Tor, near Two Bridges, a tor which is not only almost equidistant from the four stannary towns, but also almost the geographical centre of upland Dartmoor and, therefore, the mining industry. It is said that seats were hewn from the tor granite at Crockern for the parliament, but no unnatural features are visible today. One formation does look like a giant chair (and is known as the Judge's Chair or Parliament Rock) but it is, in fact, natural.

Transgressors against stannary law were imprisoned in the Stannary Gaol at Lydford, a building now (wrongly) called Lydford Castle. The gaol could also be used to imprison non-tinners, as it was against stannary law to stand in the way of mining operations. When Richard Strode, MP for Plympton, complained about mining debris in moorland rivers silting Plymouth's harbour, he was kidnapped and thrown into the Lydford gaol, only being released when he promised to stay quiet.

Strode is seen by some as the father of 'green' issues, and his imprisonment did result in legislation on free speech. It also signalled the decline in the tin miners' pre-eminence on the moor. Tin mining continued for 800 years until the early twentieth century, but today all that remains are the ruins at sites such as Eylesbarrow, Vitifer and Golden Dagger. It is an interesting sidelight on the modern view of Dartmoor that although any attempt to re-open the sites would be widely opposed, so would the removal of the evocative, even romantic, mine ruins.

The remains of Wheal Betsy mine, now in the care of the National Trust, was once an important lead mine, its furnace fired with peat cut at Walkham Head. Despite Dartmoor being famous for its tin mines, copper, lead, zinc, silver and even small quantities of iron and arsenic were also mined

The Judge's Chair on Crockern Tor

4 Land use, culture and customs

In 1239 Henry III gave Lydford with its castle and the Forest of Dartmoor to his brother Richard, the Earl of Cornwall. A century later Edward III reinforced the royal settlement by creating the Duchy of Cornwall for the benefit of his son Edward, the Black Prince, the first Duke of Cornwall.

The Duchy is still Dartmoor's largest private landowner, controlling some 30 per cent of the National Park, including both tenant farms and common land. In the seventeenth and eighteenth centuries, the Duchy authorised its tenants to create 'newtakes'. These were areas of rough moorland common which could be enclosed to increase the tenant's holding. The tenant was allowed to enclose 8 acres (3.2ha), but this was interpreted as meaning 8 acres of usable land and as a result, the newtakes were sometimes very large, blanket bog and clitter being excluded from the arithmetic. Attempts to improve the land with fertiliser and lime were a failure on the high moor, and the newtakes eventually reverted to their original form, though the remnants of enclosing walls can still occasionally be seen.

Those farms which still exist on the high moor comprise surviving newtakes together with rights over adjacent common land. The farms may also have 'inbye' fields, moorland where fertiliser

Above: Teignhead newtake wall with Fernworthy behind. The old walls provide farmers with a degree of stock control on the open moor
Right: Will Hutchings herding sheep at Yardworthy

Lynchets, Challacombe. Lynchets are terraces on sloping land formed by ploughing. The resulting strips made the land easier to cultivate. Dating lynchets is not easy but it is generally agreed that they were formed between Saxon and early medieval times

and reseeding has improved the land. At the moorland fringes, the so-called mid-moor farms comprise only inbye fields, together with rights of common, while at the edge of the National Park, most farms are too remote from the moorland commons to have any common rights. Here, however, the land is much more productive and some large-scale arable farming is possible.

As the visitor moves from the Park's boundary towards the high moor, fewer cultivated fields are seen, and the density of animals reduces as the land becomes poorer. The sheep the visitor sees will probably be Scottish Blackface, bred to withstand the fierce Highland weather and introduced to Dartmoor during the nineteenth century. Exmoor Horn and Cheviot sheep may also be seen. The cattle are also hardier northern breeds, such as Galloway and Aberdeen Angus, though the former are sometimes crossed with Herefords. In summer, South Devon cattle are sometimes brought on to the moor from their sheltered winter quarters in an enactment of the transhumance that has probably been practised more or less continuously since Neolithic times. The only other livestock the visitor is likely to see is the Dartmoor pony which, though owned and bred by moorland farmers, is semi-wild and was considered in Chapter 2.

Farming on Dartmoor is hard, the poor soil and harsh climate meaning that ewes have fewer lambs, and cultivated crops do not represent a useful addition to the farmer's income. In areas where the soil is more fertile, there is also pressure from conservationists to retain species-rich habitats, such as marginal moorland and meadows, rather than to plough for cash crops. On rough moor farms a pressure of a different kind can arise from the access agreements negotiated by the National Park Authority; sometimes walkers and riders can cause localised erosion; other problems can arise from non-caring visitors who cause litter or sheep worrying as a result of poorly controlled dogs. Subsidies from the EU's Common Agricultural Policy help – indeed, without livestock support payments, most of the upland farms could not survive – but increasingly farms have been combined to produce more cost-effective units, with a consequent decrease in the number of people working the land.

MOORLAND INDUSTRIES

Depopulation has also resulted from the loss of industries based on the moor's mineral wealth. As noted in the previous chapter, tin mining ended during the early years of the twentieth century having been a significant moorland industry for over 700 years. Apart from tin, copper, lead, zinc, silver and even iron was mined on Dartmoor, none on anything but a limited scale. Even arsenic was extracted, chiefly for use as an insecticide in the American cotton fields.

Some of the other industries which sought to exploit moorland minerals failed much quicker. The cutting of peat for fuel had been carried out for centuries – and continued until the late 1950s – but in 1847, the Zeal Tramway was built across the southern moor to Red Lake Mire where is was hoped to extract naphtha from peat for use in mothballs. The tramway was a work of art, using granite sleepers and wooden rails along which horses hauled wagons, but the venture failed after only three years – though the tramway was later restored to serve a kaolin mine. Other naphtha mines were no more successful, nor was a 1920s venture near the

Powder Mills near Postbridge. The remains of the gunpowder mill are well spread reflecting the caution of the builders who wished to reduce the chances of a major explosion. The chimney was the flue for the charcoal burning house, though it was soon found to be more economic to bring charcoal in from off the moor. The mortar used to confirm the quality of the powder by firing a standard shot can still be seen at the site

Sourton village, with Sourton Tors beyond. Note the drift lane coming in off the moor. In the nineteenth century an iceworks was established on the northern flank of the tor, where a natural spring was harnessed to run into a terrace of shallow pits. When the water froze, the ice was cut into blocks, and transported to the fish market at Plymouth

site of Meldon Reservoir. Here aplite, a rare even-grained quartz-feldspar mineral occurs, one used in the ceramic and glass industries. A bottle factory was built to exploit its presence: the factory's owners predicted it would be the biggest in the country and would make huge profits, but they were wrong, and the venture soon failed. Near Postbridge, potatoes were planted over a large acreage, with the aim of extracting starch from them. This could hardly be termed an attempt to exploit Dartmoor's mineral wealth, but the result was the same – and the venture soon failed.

A little more successful was the gunpowder mill set up on the northern moor about half-way between Postbridge and Two Bridges. The mill was built in 1844, and Dartmoor was chosen because of its ready supply of building stone and water, and also because it offered the necessary degree of isolation for a dangerous industry. The produced powder was tested by placing a measured amount in a mortar, firing a standard cannonball and confirming it had travelled a satisfactory distance. Doubtless the lack of neighbours to be annoyed by such ear-splitting tests was another reason for choosing this remote location. The site is called Powder Mills, and the remains of the mill buildings can still be seen. An equally curious use of the moor was the nineteenth-century ice factory at Sourton Tors on the northern moor. Here, shallow troughs were dug and, in winter, spring water was diverted into them. Overnight, the water froze, and the following morning the ice was collected and transported by horse-drawn cart to the railway at Meldon, then by train to Plymouth where fishermen used it to preserve their catches. Winters were much colder then, and ice was produced on many nights from October to March, but the long transportation to Plymouth allowed most of the ice to thaw, and the 'factory' soon stopped production.

More successful were the attempts to exploit the moor's most obvious feature, the granite rock of which it is composed, and a product of the weathering of that rock, china clay. Water attacks the feldspar in granite to form anhydrous silicates of aluminium and potassium. Well below the surface this decomposition is assisted by gases percolating up from deep within the earth, a process known as kaolinisation, producing a powder which, in its pure form, is called china clay. The process's name, and kaolin, the alternative name for the powder, derive from *Kao Lin*, a mountain in China where the clay was first worked. Kaolin is used to create the finest porcelain and is an important component of high-quality paper.

It is claimed that the china clay industry of south-western England was started in the eighteenth century by William Cooksworthy, a Quaker from Kingsbridge on the south Devon coast. Cooksworthy is said to have realised the potential of the kaolin deposits at Hensbarrow, near Bodmin, during a visit to Cornwall. It was an auspicious time to start a new industry based on mining – the Cornish tin industry was in decline and there was no shortage of experienced local manpower. Cooksworthy opened a factory in Plymouth and, in 1768 produced the first genuine English porcelain.

The Cornish china clay deposits are extensive, and for fifty years the industry thrived. Only in the 1830s did the need for further clay deposits persuade anyone to explore the possibility of Dartmoor having significant amounts of kaolin. The northern moor had none, but on Lee Moor, at the southern edge of the southern moor, deposits that were commercially viable were discovered, and by the mid-nineteenth century there were several mines on the moor. The kaolin is exposed by tearing away the top surface of the moor and the mineral is then either dug out and transferred to settling tanks, or washed into tanks by water sprays. In the first settling tank the heavy quartz and mica particles sink to the bottom, the purer clay solution being drawn off into another tank. In the second tank the clay particles settle out, water being drawn off and the residue being kiln-dried to produce pure kaolin.

Once the clay was used almost exclusively in the making of porcelain, but today that is only a minor usage, over 80 per cent being used in the production of paper. One of the interesting aspects of the Dartmoor industry was the use of water as a transport medium. In order to make the best use of their plant, the owners needed to bring the clay to the site cheaply and efficiently and with Dartmoor's relative abundance of water this was achieved by using gravity to transfer the clay in solution through pipes. The pipes of early clay works can still be seen in the Plym Valley near Shaugh Bridge.

The quarrying of Dartmoor granite in the way we understand the process today, as opposed to the *ad hoc* gathering of clitter for house or wall building, began in the early nineteenth century when the Haytor Quarry was opened by George Templer. George was the son of James Templer who in 1792 had been given permission to dig a canal from Bovey Tracey to the River Teign at Stover. George planned to use the canal to shift granite to Teignmouth from where it would be loaded on to ships. To transport the stone from the quarries he built a

Haytor tramway. The tramway was built by George Templer to take granite building stone from his moorland quarries to a canal at Bovey Tracey from where it was shipped by barge to Teignmouth. The stone which was horse-hauled was then loaded on to ships. The high costs of moving Dartmoor granite eventually closed most quarries

GRANITE COBBLES

One other use of Dartmoor granite deserves a mention – the making of setts, as cobblestones were known locally during the late nineteenth century. The cobbles were made on 'bankers', a granite bench supported by granite uprights, the makers being paid 1d (one old penny) per sett. A good sett maker could produce about forty in a day, earning about 17p in today's money. The setts were used to construct roads in towns from Plymouth to Exeter.

Top: Granite seat, Dunnabridge Pound

Above: Foggin Tor quarry buildings

tramway which used granite rails rather than iron, and had the flanges on the rails rather than on the carriage wheels, as was more usually the case. The stone from Templer's quarries was used for the arches of London Bridge and the columns of the old British Library.

Templer's competitors for the production of Dartmoor granite building stone were the Swell Tor/Foggintor quarries, close to Princetown, opened by Thomas Tyrwhitt, who was famous for the construction of both Princetown and the nearby prison. Tyrwhitt also built a railway to transport his stone, but it took much longer to complete than he had planned and to his great annoyance his quarries lost the contract for London Bridge to the quarries of Haytor and Aberdeen.

To the west of Tyrwhitt's quarries, Heckwood, near Vixen Tor, supplied the stone for Plymouth's breakwater. Between the two sites is Merrivale Quarry, the last working quarry on the moor which started life in 1875 as Tor Quarry. Merrivale stone was used to create the war memorial on the Falkland Islands.

Some present-day land uses of Dartmoor today can be controversial in a National Park. There are eight reservoirs within the Park, though six were built before the National Park was designated. The Avon Dam was completed in 1957 and the Meldon scheme was chosen in 1968 on the grounds of cost against another site outside the National Park. In 1970 a proposal to build another reservoir inside the Park was rejected.

In 1919, the Duchy of Cornwall planted 5,000 acres (2024ha) at Fernworthy with conifers, the first of several large conifer forests on the moor. Today the three large plantations of Fernworthy, Soussons Down and Bellever are owned by the Forestry Commission, with other plantations in private hands. In an effort to limit the impact of conifer plantations on the moorland landscape, its wildlife and archaeological sites, the National Park Authority has an agreement with the relevant owners on the afforestation of undeveloped land.

The third use is perhaps the most incongruous – the presence of the military and the practice of live firing on the northern moor. Military manoeuvres have been carried out on the moor since the beginning of the nineteenth century, a licence for permanent occupation being granted by the Duchy of Cornwall in 1895. At present the Ministry of Defence controls (by ownership, lease or licence) about 33,000 acres (13,352ha or about 14 per cent of the National Park's area) of the northern moor. Live firing and 'dry' (no live ammunition) training are carried out, a red flag system being used to exclude the public during the live firing. Several inquiries into the military use of the moor have been undertaken, that in 1975–76 concluding that live firing represented a hazard to the moor's archaeological sites, its wildlife and landscape and restricted public access. Presently the National Park Authority is resisting further capital investment in the military facilities and seeking an end to live firing, although the modernisation of the Willsworthy range was agreed by the Secretary of State for the Environment in 1981. Visitors intending to walk on the northern moor should consult National Park Visitor Centres for times of live firing. But at all times, if red flags are flying by day, or there are red lights by night, do not enter the ranges.

Above: Merrivale Quarry opened (as Tor Quarry) in the late nineteenth century and closed in 1997. In 1903 it set a record by producing over 1,500 tons of stone in a single firing, some of which was used for work on London Bridge. When the bridge was sold to the Americans the granite blocks were re-dressed at Merrivale. Merrivale stone was used for the war memorial on the Falkland Islands

Left: Fernworthy Reservoir. In times of drought the old bridges spanning the South Teign river reveal themselves

Above: Pat Coaker with her Widecombe Whiteface sheep
Left: Widecombe-in-the-Moor. Although mistakenly thought to mean 'wide coombe' as in 'wide valley', the name derives from withies that once grew along the valley bottom

MOORLAND FOLKLORE

The decline in the Dartmoor industries, tin mining, quarrying and the shorter-lived ventures corresponded with the increase in tourism which followed the rise in the Romantic movement in Britain and Europe. The upland areas of Britain – nature in the raw peopled with 'noble savages' – appealed to the Romantics.

The Lake District, home of Wordsworth and Ruskin, was the prime area, but Dartmoor had its share of visitors, even if its blanket bogs more often inspired dread rather than the awe of Lakeland's shapely peaks and rock faces. The loss of local people meant a loss of the moor's folklore, and we can only be grateful for the Rev Sabine Baring-Gould who wrote down many folk songs and others who wrote down some of the folk stories, before they were finally lost for good. The moor's stories, like the moor itself, are dark and forbidding – though to be fair most folk tales deal with such things as they tend to stay in the memory longer than more cheerful events. On Dartmoor, as elsewhere, many of the stories are local versions of traditional supernatural tales, but some are entirely moor-based and almost certainly grounded in fact.

Of the local tales, the best known is that of Tom Pearce's mare on its way to Widecombe Fair under the burden of six named individuals, an un-named narrator, Uncle Tom Cobley and all. Widecombe Fair still exists – it is held in September – and the old song is almost certainly based on a real event in which a number of farmers, the worse for drink after a convivial day, rode a horse to an exhausted death. After that, it requires only a little embroidery for Tom Pearce's mare to appear 'ghostly white' on the local moor.

Another true Widecombe-in-the-Moor incident has been similarly embroidered. In 1638 during the service on Sunday 21 October, at the height of a fierce storm a 'bolt of fire' knocked one of the pinnacles off the church tower. The pinnacle fell through the roof and four of the congregation were killed, though a contemporary record claims they were killed not by the pinnacle, but by a fiery ball that passed through the church at the same time. Was this an example of the poorly-understood ball lightning? Local legend claims that Jan Reynolds, a local man, borrowed money from the Devil in order to pay gambling debts and was due to repay it on that Sunday. Finding Jan in church, the Devil hauled him out, and as the pair flew into the air, a trailing foot (or cloven hoof) dislodged the pinnacle.

Equally embroidered is the tale of Richard Cabell, a seventeenth-century squire of Buckfastleigh. He is said to have bred a pack of huge, fierce dogs and hunted them on the moor, little caring whether the quarry was deer, fox or one of his tenants. When he died in 1677, the locals erected a tomb with a heavy top slab and an iron grille to prevent his spirit from haunting the neighbourhood. In reality Cabell does not seem to have been particularly wicked, there even being a suggestion that his story only surfaced after publication of *The Hound of the Baskervilles*, perhaps in an effort to cash in on its notoriety.

A much older tale is associated with Childe's Tomb near Foxtor Mires on the southern moor. Here a medieval cross has been added to a prehistoric burial mound, and the story maintains that the cross commemorates a local hunter. The man became separated from his hunting colleagues on a winter's day and was eventually lost in a violent snowstorm. Overcome by the cold, the man killed his horse and crawled inside its corpse for warmth and shelter. But his blood-soaked clothes soon froze and by the time he was found, he had also died of cold. One version of the story claims his name was Amos Childe, but another version pushes the tale back to Saxon times, claiming the hunter was a *cild*, a leader.

Childe's Tomb is named for one of Dartmoor's most tragic stories, that of a hunter lost in a vicious snow-storm who killed his horse to shelter within its body

Childe's story is a sad one, as is that of Kitty Jay. She was the daughter of a tenant farmer who fell in love with the landowner's son. Seduced by tales of love and marriage, Kitty spent a long night of passion with the boy, only to be told the following morning that he would never marry such a low-born girl. Kitty went home and hanged herself in her father's barn. As was the custom, Kitty was not allowed a Christian burial, and was buried at a cross-roads so her spirit, confused by the number of roads, would not wander. Years later, wanting to know the truth of the tale a man excavated the grave and found it did indeed contain the skeleton of a young woman. The man created the grave with its simple headstone that still stands by the old cross-roads. There the story would have ended, but it is said that flowers are regularly placed on the grave by a ghostly hand, and that those who stay at the cross-roads at night to try to watch are driven away by unseen terrors before the flowers arrive.

Claimed to be as true as the story of Jay's Grave is an incident which occurred in the Warren House Inn, on the B3212 north-east of Postbridge. A traveller spending the night there during a prolonged storm was curious about a huge chest in his room. On opening it he discovered a body inside. He ran to the landlord to report the murder, but was even more alarmed to be told not to worry as it was 'only father'. The old man had been salted down because the storm had prevented him being taken along the Lich Way to Lydford.

More curious than the above tales, because it seems impossible that it can be based on any truth, is the story associated with the Grey Wethers stone circle near Sittaford Tor. It is claimed that wives suspected of unfaithfulness were taken across the moor to Cranmere Pool and forced to bathe there, then taken to Grey Wethers. There the women were forced to kneel in front of a stone: if it fell on them they were guilty, if not they were innocent. The tale maintains that the falling stone would crush the women, but the circle's stones seem hardly big enough, and the tale has much more intriguing contradictions – how it could have survived if a stone never actually fell at exactly the right moment? And what does the large number of fallen stones say about Dartmoor wives?

Jay's Grave lies in the parish of Manaton. It is said to be that of Kitty Jay, a poor farmer's daughter who was betrayed by a squire's son. It is said that the flowers on the grave are replaced each night by a ghostly hand

Cranmere Pool is also the site of one of the moor's most interesting haunting tales. Benjamin (Binjie) Gayer, Mayor of Okehampton in the seventeenth century, is said to have been hanged on Hangingstone Hill for sheep stealing, and his spirit was required to empty Cranmere Pool with a sieve. When the clever Binjie lined his sieve with a sheepskin, the punishment was changed to weaving the sand at the bottom of the pool into a rope.

In addition to Binjie Gayer's haunting of Cranmere Pool, Dartmoor has a whole collection of ghosts, usually black dogs or phantom riders. Most are malevolent, but the White Lady, for whom the waterfall at the southern end of the Lydford Gorge is named, is benevolent. If the Lady appears to someone unfortunate enough to fall down the cliff over which the waterfall tumbles, then they will not drown in the pool at its base. However, it's a long drop and a shallow pool, so the fall might kill you first.

The dark side of the moor is most readily seen in the tales which associate the devil with certain landmarks. Wistman's Wood is said to be named for the 'Wisht' hounds that the Devil used to hunt the moor for the souls of sinners. The hounds chased the souls to the copse where they would become trapped by the boulders and bent branches – easy pickings for the pursuing dogs. The Devil also names the Dewerstone ('dewer' being a local name for him), and the hounds are said to occasionally chase sinners over the cliff at the base of which the Devil would pick off their souls.

One tale says that an old farmer met the Devil carrying a sack away from the base of the rock. In failing light and with failing eyesight, the farmer did not recognise the Devil and, assuming he was a hunter, asked whether he had had a successful day. The Devil laughed and thrust the bag at the former telling him he was welcome to the catch. The gleeful old man hurried home and called to his wife to come and see what he had got. When the pair emptied the sack it contained the broken body of their son.

The open moor is not only the haunt of the Devil, but of pixies and witches. Stories of pixies might be associated with the natural phenomenon of *ignis fatuus*,

The Dewerstone. Dewer is a local name for the devil who is said to chase sinners across the moor with a pack of ferocious hounds causing them to fall from the rock so that he can pick off their souls

the methane-fuelled will o' the wisp whose pale blue, flicking flame was likely to convince any superstitious traveller that they had seen the fires of the little people. As lately as the 1960s a walker claimed to have seen a pixie on Fur Tor.

Will o' the wisps might have been seen as the work of witches, too, though there is plenty of evidence to suggest that any village's eccentric old woman was likely to have been thought to be a witch. Bowerman's Nose, one of the moor's most distinctive tors, is said to have been created by witchcraft. Bowerman was a hunter who one day came across a coven of witches and ran shouting through their midst, terrifying them. Days later he was caught by the witches who encased him in stone. When his family came looking for him, he could see them, but they could not hear him or recognise him in his granite overcoat. In time they gave up the search, but Bowerman stills looks out across the moor, trapped for eternity.

BEATING THE BOUNDS

Beating the Bounds is an ancient ceremony, probably medieval in origin. The parishioners walked the parish boundary, the beating being the symbolic touching of boundary stones or other markers with a rod. As the parish became less important within communities. Beatings became less frequent and eventually died out altogether. On Dartmoor, as elsewhere, the idea was revived during the twentieth century, more to give the parishioners a good day out than for any original purpose. Lustleigh, on the eastern side of the moor, revived their Beating in 1924, at first as an annual event. Since 1970 however the Beating has been five-yearly. The parish boundary is over 20 miles (32km) so the walk is accomplished over two days of the Whitsun Bank Holiday weekend. Most of Dartmoor's parishes have now also revived the custom.

The boundary of the Dartmoor Forest is known to have been Beaten in 1240, the boundaries then measuring about 50 miles (80km). The relatively new parish of Dartmoor Forest, whose boundaries approximate to the old Forest boundary, revived the custom, but Beat only part of the long boundary.

THE COMPLETE DARTMOOR TALE

A bloodthirsty tale surrounds Vixen Tor, once the home of the witch Vixana. She lived on the bodies of those sucked down by the bog below the tor, conjuring up thick mists to ensure they would lose the safe path. The last noise the lost traveller would hear would be Vixana's gleeful cackle. But one day Vixana conjured a mist around a traveller who had a ring given him by a grateful moorland elf he had saved from another bog. The ring allowed him to see through the moor's mists and, if he twisted it, to become invisible. On the far side of the bog, still safely on the path, he heard Vixana's laugh and climbed on to the tor. Twisting the ring to become invisible, he crept up on the witch and hurled her to her death at the tor's base.

Vixana's story links the supernatural to the leg-devouring potential of Dartmoor's bogs. Sir Arthur Conan Doyle is said to have based Grimpen Mire in The Hound of the Baskervilles *on Foxtor Mires, but he must also have been aware of other Dartmoor legends too, as the tale weaves in nightmarish, ghostly dogs as well as the essence of Vixana's story. In that way, it might be argued, the story is the complete Dartmoor tale.*

Above left: Beating the bounds at Throwleigh
Left: Vixen Tor. The tor was the home of a wicked witch who conjured mists to confuse travellers who then drowned in the nearby bog. She was defeated by a traveller who had a magic stone

DARTMOOR PRISON

The military use of Dartmoor's northern moor seems a curious use of land in a National Park to many visitors. But others would argue that even stranger is the existence of a prison. The grim, forbidding, ruthlessly functional prison at Princetown was the work of one of Dartmoor's most remarkable characters.

Thomas Tyrwhitt, an Essex man, became a friend of the Prince of Wales when the two were at Oxford University. In 1786, Tyrwhitt was appointed as auditor for the Duchy of Cornwall and saw Dartmoor for the first time. He decided that what the moor needed was a town at its heart, its folk taming the wilderness to the Prince's (and his own) profit. He built the town, calling it Prince's Town after his patron (though its inhabitants rapidly shortened this to Princetown). Despite Tyrwhitt's enthusiasm, Dartmoor would not be tamed, and the future for his town looked bleak.

But Tyrwhitt had arrived on Dartmoor at the time of the Napoleonic Wars and, seeing the disquiet about the conditions of the French prisoners of war in the prison hulks at Plymouth, he proposed the building of a prison at his new town. The prison was built by French prisoners and some American prisoners from the War of Independence, and took much longer than planned because of the weather and the difficulties of transport. It was finally opened in 1809 and has been in use ever since.

Today, though visitors are discouraged from lingering anywhere near the prison, it is still a landmark which draws the curious. In Princetown sales of postcards of it sell almost as well as those of other, more conventional, moorland beauty spots. Presumably many arrive with a simple message 'Wish you were here' followed by a '?' or '!' as appropriate.

The area around the prison is also the scene of one of the moor's gentlest hauntings. David Davies was sent to the prison in 1879, soon becoming a trustee who worked as a shepherd on the nearby moor. When his release date came he begged to be allowed to stay on as a shepherd, but was refused. He therefore re-offended to ensure his return to the prison and his flock. For fifty years, until his death in 1919, he remained a prisoner and a shepherd. Now on misty nights his ghost, clad in prisoners' uniform, is said to be seen wandering among the sheep.

5 Recreation

Top: Herding cattle on Haytor Down
Above: National Park Information
Centre at Postbridge

Opposite: Sorting the ponies,
Merrivale Pound

At the heart of the National Park is an area of over 91,500 acres (37,044ha) of common land. The name is something of a misnomer, as all common land is actually owned by someone, with rights to its use (for grazing, peat cutting and so on) being granted to commoners – people who own or work land adjacent to the common land. The Commons Registration Act of 1965 set up a national Common Land Register with details of ownership, commoners and the nature of their rights. On Dartmoor there are over 8,000 commoners (though in practice only about 1,500 exercise their rights) on common land owned by fifty-four different owners. The rights these commoners have include grazing – the most frequently exercised, for sheep, cattle and ponies; turbary (the right to cut turf – ie peat – for fuel for domestic purposes); estovers (the right to take branches for house repairs or domestic fuel); pannage (the right to feed pigs on acorns or beech mast), and certain rights to take stone.

Public access to common land was not guaranteed by the 1965 Act and the national register. Prior to the act such access was *de facto*, as the public had been using common land for recreation for centuries. However, such *de facto* access could potentially be revoked by the landowner. Further, the medieval system of appointed officials, known as reeves, who regulated the use of common land, had lapsed and the commoners themselves sought assistance from the National Park Authority to reintroduce a control system.

Consequently, after several years of negotiation, the Dartmoor Commons Act became law in 1985. After its enactment, the Dartmoor Commoners' Council was set up to regulate the activities of the commoners so as to maintain the health of the moor and the animals grazing it. The Act also established a legal right of access on foot and on horseback for the purposes of recreation and allowed the establishment of the Dartmoor Commons Bylaws, which regulate the behaviour of the public on the commons. Though this sounds authoritarian, the byelaws are far from Draconian, merely applying common sense to access in order to maintain the landscape and wildlife habitats. Thus, the bylaws limit vehicle access to the commons, camping, the lighting of fires, and cover such things as the control of dogs, the protection of walls and fences, and disturbance the wildlife. Copies of the full list of bylaws are available at National Information Information Centres.

Legal access to Dartmoor's common land, access agreements over other moorland areas, together with public rights of way across private land, give visitors excellent opportunities to explore the National Park, and the Labour Government's

THE MILITARY ON DARTMOOR

The Ministry of Defence has three ranges (Okehampton, Willsworthy and Merrivale) on the northern moor on which live firing of shells, mortars and bullets takes place. A leaflet is available from National Park Information Centres which show the extent of these ranges, and they are marked on the ground by flag poles and range boundary notices. On days when there is live firing, red flags are flown from the poles; if the firing is at night, red lights are shown. A list of live firing times is available from Information Centres and is published in the local press. There are also phone numbers which can be called for details and Information Centres have a list of these numbers. In general, there is no live firing at most weekends, on public holidays nor during August, but anyone intending to go out on the northern moor should always check beforehand and watch for the flags.

As well as live firing, 'dry training' also takes place on the northern ranges, and on the Cramber/Combshead and Ringmoor ranges on the southern moor. Dry training includes the use of pyrotechnics and blanks which, though noisy, are not dangerous. On days when live firing has been advertised, if the red flags are not flying by 9am (April to September) or 10am (October to March), then firing has been cancelled. Dry training may still take place however, so always take care.

When visitors are exploring the moorland within the ranges, a local bylaw forbids digging for, or collecting, any metal objects. Common sense will also tell you that such activities are not a good idea – projectiles have been known to not detonate on impact.

recent promise to extend public access to all open country will further increase these opportunities to enjoy the moor. Open access, however, brings its own problems, the greatest of which is erosion of the moor.

Dartmoor is a fragile landscape, and its vegetation is easily destroyed by walkers, mountain bikes and horses riders (and grazing animals and farm vehicles too). The vegetation takes time to re-establish, and if it fails to do so, the exposed soil can be trampled, causing gullies to form. In wet weather the gullies can become muddy, resulting in walkers and riders finding a different route and repeating the process. To combat erosion the National Park Authority has introduced the 'Moor Care, Less Wear' scheme, which lays down simple guidelines to minimise the impact of public access on the moor. Copies of these guidelines are also available at National Park Information Centres. Visitors will also see 'Take Moor Care' signs prominently displayed on access roads to the moor. A 40mph speed limit has been introduced on all cross-moor roads. In 1995, more than 300 sheep, cattle and ponies were killed on Dartmoor's roads, and hopefully the speed limit will reduce the toll.

WALKING

Walking is by far the most popular way of exploring Dartmoor, and access to the common land, and access agreement areas, together with a further 372 miles (600km) of rights of way within the National Park and additional permissive paths, along which landowners have given permission for walkers to cross their land, allow almost unlimited possibilities.

A leaflet published by the National Park Authority gives a code of conduct for walkers on the moor. This covers not only personal safety – where poor weather, including mists, can occur quickly, disorientating the walker – but also certain requests. Chief of these is for dog owners to control their dogs so that grazing animals and wildlife are not disturbed. This is particularly important during the spring when moorland birds are nesting, and grazing animals are giving birth.

Walkers are also asked to follow existing paths to avoid erosion and, where possible, to follow hard tracks. On the northern moor there are a number of peat passes cut through the blanket bog, which should be used to minimise erosion of the bog. The passes were cut by Frank Phillpotts, a Victorian gentleman, to help moormen but chiefly hunters, to travel more easily across difficult sections of the moor. Phillpotts cut down through the peat to the granite sub-strata, creating a good path for horses. His half-dozen or so passes are all marked at each end by memorial stones/plaques erected by his brother and son.

A famous Dartmoor walk is the Ten Tors, first held in the 1960s. This is a weekend challenge walk for groups of walkers held annually in May, the actual line of the walk varying each year. The timing, during the nesting season of moorland birds, causes some concern.

For those walkers who do not feel they have the necessary experience to tackle the open moor, or who would like to know more about the history or wildlife of certain areas, an extensive programme of guided walks is organised each year by the National Park Authority. Details of the dates, start times and routes of these walks are published in *The Dartmoor Visitor*, a free newspaper available at National Park Information Centres.

LETTERBOXING

In the nineteenth century, trips to wilderness areas became the vogue among the leisured classes and Dartmoor's Cranmere Pool became a popular destination, with local folk acting as guides. In 1854 one of these guides, James Perrott, built a cairn at the pool. Inside it he placed a glass jar into which his clients could drop their visiting cards, and a visitors' book which they could sign. When the guided tours ended, other walkers replaced Perrott's jar and book. Then, in 1937, the *Western Morning News* raised money to erect a stone box. This still stands at the pool, its door opening to reveal a rubber stamp for the use of 'letterboxers'. The name letterbox came from the early use of the Cranmere box, a walker would bring a self-addressed card to the pool and exchange it for the one left by the last visitor, posting that on his return to 'civilisation'. The recipient would then marvel (or not) at the time taken for his card to reach him.

Further letterboxes followed at Ducks Pool in 1938 and Fur Tor in 1951 (there was already another at Taw Marsh, put there in 1894). All these locations are relatively inaccessible, a degree of commitment being required to reach them.

Opposite: Soldiers on the moor at High Willhays
Left: Bennet's Cross

Pages 88–9: Hound Tor and Greator Rocks

In time, many more letterboxes were added, with groups growing up who used the placing and finding of the boxes to enhance their enjoyment of the moor. There are now many thousands of letterboxes on the moor. Such a number gave the National Park Authority cause for concern, because many of the boxes were deliberately hidden, and the hiding and the subsequent searching by other letterboxers damaged wildlife habitats. As a result, a code of practice has been published (a leaflet on letterboxing, including the code of practice, is available from Information Centres) which defines the type of letterbox which can be used, where it should be sited and, most importantly, the 'no go' areas for boxes.

Today letterboxing is a semi-organised sport under the direction of the Dartmoor 100 Club. Authorised boxes have visitors' books which letterboxers stamp with their own stamps, and stamps which the letterboxer uses to stamp his/her record sheet. Collectors of 100 stamps qualify to join the club.

Sanders at Lettaford, a Dartmoor longhouse which is now available as holiday accommodation

HORSE RIDING

Horse riding can be enjoyed on the open moorland because the Dartmoor Commons Act, 1985 ensured open access to common land for those on horseback as well as those on foot. Public bridleways, byways and certain permitted routes where landowners have given permission for riders to cross their land, are also available to horse riders.

Riding can cause erosion of the moor. There may be fewer riders, but a single horse can cause much more damage than a single walker, especially if ridden fast over soft ground. The National Park Authority publishes a code of conduct for riders available from National Park Information Centres, which also gives tips on safety for riders. Because of the nature of the ground, it is recommended that crash helmets are worn.

CYCLING

The public roads that cross high Dartmoor are ideal for cycling for although the moor is an upland area, it is also a relatively flat plateau with limited climbs. Cyclists are also allowed on public bridleways and byways, on some Forestry Commission roads and certain cycle tracks. The latter include the Plym Valley Cycle Way, the Plymouth-Okehampton length of the National Cycle Network, and the trackbed of the disused Princetown railway. The National Park Authority is continuously seeking to improve access for cyclists on other routes.

There is, however, no legal right of way for cyclists on public footpaths or on open moorland. The Dartmoor Commons Act, 1985 allows access on foot or on horseback, but not on cycles. Off-road cycling (mountain biking) has become increasingly popular in recent years, but indiscriminate riding can antagonise landowners, walkers and horseriders. Fast cycling over soft moorland can cause considerable damage and should be avoided at all times. The National Park Authority has issued a code of conduct for cyclists, and new routes and opportunities are currently being identified. Further information is available from National Park Information Centres.

The National Park Authority also issues a series of leaflets – Off Road cycling with Moor Care and Less Wear – with details of permitted routes.

Sunset over Bonehill Rocks

CLIMBING

Dartmoor's tors are ideal for climbers – particularly those willing to lose skin from their hands as the granite is very rough – though the lack of height of many tors is something of a drawback. Only at Haytor/Low Man and the Dewerstone does the granite gain any real height. However, at other places, particularly Hound Tor and Vixen Tor, the short but steep outcrops offer real challenges.

Though the climber would seem to offer little chance of damage to the tors, climbing does pose a threat to the landscape. The indiscriminate use of fixed belays, particular at the top of tors set into, rather than on top of, hillsides, can cause soil erosion, and belaying or abseiling from trees can cause damage to the few substantial trees on the moor. To counteract these threats the National Park Authority has issued a code of conduct for climbers which is this is available from National Park Information Centres.

A guide to climbing on Dartmoor's tors (and to the cliffs of South Devon) is published by Cordee. Note that climbing is not allowed on all tors – National Park Information Centres have lists of the accessible ones.

CANOEING

Heavy winter rain often creates challenging canoe courses on the larger Dartmoor rivers. However, there is no public right of navigation on virtually all Britain's non-tidal waterways, and even where rights do exist, there is not necessarily a right of access across land to the riverbank. Increasingly such access, if it exists, has been granted only to British Canoe Union members. For information on access to Dartmoor's rivers please contact the Head of Recreation at the National Park Authority or the Local Access Officer of the British Canoe Union.

EASY-GOING

Under the heading Easy-Going Dartmoor, the National Park Authority and the Countryside Access Group for Dartmoor have produced a booklet with information on a number of walks specifically designed for disabled or less mobile visitors, those with babies in prams or young children in push-chairs. The booklet also has information on horse riding centres which cater for the disabled, and the position of toilets for the disabled. Large print copies of the booklet are available for the visually handicapped; please ask for a copy in advance of your visit.

The National Park Authority has also issued a code of conduct for canoeists which is available from National Park Information Centres. The leaflet also includes advice on personal safety both in the canoe and in the water, should you be unlucky enough to capsize, and advice on how to avoid infection from water-borne pollutants and diseases.

FISHING

Dartmoor's eight reservoirs are controlled by South-West Water which maintains fish stocks and regulate fishing. Information on the species of fish (rainbow or brown trout) at each reservoir and the permits required to fish them can be obtained from South-West Water (see Information). In addition, opportunities for river fishing are many, particularly on the Duchy of Cornwall's River Dart fishery. Leaflets are available at local information offices.

SOME SUGGESTED WALKS

The following walks are designed to give the active visitor a taste of the varied landscapes and history of the National Park.

Exploring the Dewerstone and the Plym Valley, a 4½mile (7km) walk from the car park beside Shaugh Bridge takes about two hours. Follow a path – known as the 'Pipe Track' after the pipeline which brought china clay from Lee Moor to the Shaugh Bridge drying kilns – through the beautiful Plym Valley woods to Cadover Bridge.

East Dart waterfall. The waterfall is formed by the layered nature of the granite, harder and softer bands of stone being eroded at different rates. The fall, close to Sandy Hole Pass to the north of Postbridge, though remote, is one of the high moor's most popular targets for walkers

From the bridge, turn up on to Wigford Down and by the edge of Cadworthy Wood, passing through a hillfort and continuing to the top of the Dewerstone. Follow the path through Dewerstone Wood to a narrow path which leads towards the River Meavy and its confluence with the Plym, crossing a footbridge over the river to regain the start.

The second suggested walk visits the famous Grey Wethers stone circle from the National Park Information Centre in Postbridge. The walk is about 8½miles (13.5km) and takes about three hours. **This walk lies within one of the Army's Dartmoor Firing Ranges, so please read the section on the ranges before setting out.**

The walk follows the B3212 towards Moretonhampstead, crossing the bridge over the East Dart River, turning left on a waymarked path past Ringhill Farm to reach the river. Passing Hartyland Farm the path reaches open country, where the river is followed the river until it reaches Lade Hill Brook which runs into the river. Heading almost due north and climbing gently though the boggy valley, you will eventually reach the Grey Wethers stone circle. Turn west to Sittaford Tor and reach the high point of Winney's Down. Follow the Marsh Hill Peat Pass and then go south to reach the East Dart River. Follow the river through Sandy Hole Pass and continue past a fine waterfall to reach the outward route.

The megalithic sites of Merrivale are the objective on the next 4-mile (6.5km) walk from the Four Winds car park on the southern side of the B3357, about 3 miles (5km) west of Two Bridges.

Head south-west, then west across the moor following a leat to reach the megalithic sites. From the car park end of the stone rows, head south-east following the row of cairns, then walk across open moor to reach a 'T/A' stone, marking the old route from Tavistock to Ashburton. Continue southwards to cross Long Ash Brook, follow a wall, and maintain direction when it ends to reach the old trackbed of the Plymouth to Dartmoor Railway. Follow the old trackbed around King's Tor, forking right then left along the main trackbed, and descending to reach a raised causeway through another quarry.

The line from Princetown is followed with Swell Tor on the left, and Foggin Tor on the right, crossing the moor and then rounding King's Tor to regain the point at which the trackbed was reached. Reverse the outward route to regain the start.

Bowerman's Nose, a stunning granite formation on Hayne Down near Manaton

Some of the most impressive moorland features of Hound Tor, Becky Falls and Bowerman's Nose are visited on a 7-mile (11km) walk from the car park at Swallerton Gate, which takes about three hours.

Walk uphill to the twin tors known as Hound Tor. Follow the grassy avenue between them towards the clear ruins of the medieval village. Continue with Greator Rocks off to the right, over a clapper bridge to reach a fork near Leighon. Turn right, for Upper Terrace Drive, to an unfenced minor road going steeply downhill to reach a road junction. Turn right to reach the car park for Becky Falls to the right, and the entrance to the falls a little further on to the left.

Follow the path from the gift shop, crossing the bridge and turning left (the falls are reached by turning right here). Follow the public footpath to reach the Kestor Inn. Opposite the inn, take the turning for Southcott to reach a crossroads at Hayne Cross. Go straight over, following a lane onto open moorland and the climb over Hayne Down to reach Bowerman's Nose.

Go downhill to the unfenced minor road and then trn left to return to Swallerton Gate.

The mythical moorland features of Siward's Cross, Childe's Tomb and Foxtor Mires can be reached by a 5-mile (8km) walk starting and finishing at Whiteworks, a hamlet reached by a minor road from Princetown. The walk crosses open moorland and should not be attempted in poor weather or without map, compass and adequate equipment.

From Whiteworks, follow the road back towards Princetown, turning left to walk to Siward's Cross. At the cross, follow the Abbot's Way past the ruins of Nun's Cross Farm. Heads uphill towards Crane Hill and then follow the Black Lane Peat Pass east through the tin mine debris in Fox Tor Girt to reach the twin tors of Fox Tor.

Now head north, descending to go through a gate in a wall, soon reaching Childe's Tomb. Return to the wall and turn right (west) to reach a track heading north-west around the edge of Foxtor Mires back towards Whiteworks.

6 Exploring the Park

Ashburton is a former stannary town and coach stop for the Exeter to Plymouth stagecoach. It is now (thankfully, but ironically) bypassed by coaches on the same route. The town still elects officials to a Saxon leet court (each November) and retains the ceremonies of ale tasting and bread weighing (in July)

ASHBURTON

One of the four Dartmoor stannary towns – and the most important of the four during the sixteenth century – Ashburton is a charming place, now thankfully bypassed by the A38 dual carriageway. A walk around the town is worthwhile to see the slate-hung fronts of many buildings, a local speciality. The hardware shop in North Street was formerly the Mermaid Inn where General Fairfax, the Roundhead leader, stayed during the Civil War. During the Napoleonic wars, many French prisoners of war stayed in the town – one is buried near the base of the church tower – and the nearby willow is said to have grown from a cutting taken on St Helena.

Ashburton is one of only a handful of English towns which retains the Saxon office of Portreeve (a local representative of the monarch) and a court leet with a Bread Weigher, Ale Taster and Tree Inspector, among other unlikely officers. Well worth visiting is the local museum and the historic St Lawrence Chapel (from May–September).

BECKY FALLS

Becky (or Becka) Falls are actually a tumble rather than a vertical fall, created by the undercutting of the moor's metamorphic rock. The woodland around the falls is a haven for wildflowers, birds and butterflies making the falls a justifiably popular tourist spot.

BELSTONE

This pretty little village is grouped around a green on which stand the old stocks. Nearby is St Mary's Church, originally built in the fifteenth century but rebuilt in the 1880s. The old Zion Chapel, built in 1841, is now the post office. Close to the village is the Nine Maidens stone circle.

BOVEY TRACEY

This pleasant, airy town on the River Bovey lies outside the National Park, but is worth visiting for its church and tourist attractions. The church is a fine granite building, extensively restored in Victorian times, but with several medieval survivals inside. The tourist sites include the House of Marbles at the Teign Valley Glassworks (which has what is claimed to be the world's largest collection of marbles, as well as games and a pottery museum, and where glassmaking can be watched) and the Riverside Mill, a showroom of the the Devon Guild of Craftsmen. Parke, an early nineteenth-century house to the west of the town, houses the Dartmoor National Park Authority's headquarters. It, too, lies just outside the National Park.

BRIDFORD

At the north-eastern tip of the National Park, beyond the Kennick Reservoir complex, the village of Bridford lies in hilly country. The church, unusually dedicated to St Thomas-à-Becket, has an early sixteenth-century rood screen, a remarkable survival. Equally rare is the farmhouse of Bridford Barton which dates, in part, from the early fourteenth century. Close to Bridford is Christow, a village in an equally hilly position with a fine seventeenth-century granite church.

BUCKFAST ABBEY

The abbey was founded (or perhaps re-founded) in 1018 by Aethelweard, an Earl under King Cnut, for Benedictine monks, but became a Cistercian house in 1147. After the Dissolution, the abbey buildings were used as a convenient local quarry, but in 1882, the site was offered to the Roman Catholic church. A new abbey was built by a team of just four monks using manual rope hoists to raise the stone. The church, with its elegant, soaring lines, was consecrated in 1932 and can be visited daily. The site has a restaurant, a book shop and a gift shop which sells, among other things, the famous Buckfast honey and tonic wine.

BUCKFASTLEIGH

Buckfastleigh is a delightful Devonian town, virtually untouched by tourism despite nearby Buckfast Abbey being one of the county's most visited sites. The town grew prosperous on woollen mills and leather tanning, the mills powered by the River Mardle, and the tanning industry using bark from local oak trees. To the east of the town is the terminal station of the South Devon Railway, the Old Dart Valley Railway, closed in 1962 but restored by enthusiasts.

View from Higher Tor, near Belstone, looking south

Buckfast Abbey. Despite its medieval style the abbey was built in the 1930s, though on the site of a much older monastery. The abbey, one of Britain's few monasteries, is famous for its honey and tonic wine

Opposite: (top) Buckland-in-the-Moor. There is evidence of a Celtic settlement here, and there was probably a Saxon church long before the present church which, with its sturdy tower, was built in the fifteenth century; (below) Castle Drogo and the Teign Gorge

Close to the station is Buckfast Butterflies and the Dartmoor Otter Sanctuary. Here a tropical rain forest has been recreated within which a number of typical butterfly species breed.

The old church is on a hill and dates to the thirteenth century and is well known for Squire Cabell's tomb (see Chapter 4). Sadly on 21 July 1992, an arson attack resulted in the church being almost completely destroyed, and it is unlikely to be rebuilt.

BUCKLAND-IN-THE-MOOR

Much less visited but every bit as attractive as its near 'in-the-Moor' neighbour, Widecombe, Buckland is a lovely place, a collection of thatched cottages overlooking the woodland of Holne Chase. The early fourteenth-century church looks out across the River Webburn which joins the River Dart close to the village. The church has a fine medieval rood screen with painted figures and panels, but is perhaps most notable for the modern clock face on which MY DEAR MOTHER replaces the expected figures.

CASTLE DROGO

The curious name of the castle derives from Drogo, a grandson of Richard, Duke of Normandy, the first Norman lord. Drogo was also called Drew and gave his name to nearby Drewsteignton. The castle itself is much younger, built by Edwin

Lutyens for Julius Drewe, a grocery millionaire who claimed descent from the Norman Drew. The castle was begun in 1910, but the war and the shortages which followed it meant it was not finished until 1925. Julius Drewe died in 1931. The National Trust has owned the castle since 1974. Inside, it is a mixture of the austere and the sumptuous. Outside, there are excellent gardens.

CHAGFORD

Chagford was one of Dartmoor's four stannary towns. Its relative isolation means that traffic has not spoiled its delightful centre, dominated by the 'pepperpot' market house, dating from the mid-nineteenth century and clearly modelled on the Abbot's Kitchen at Glastonbury. Look out, too, for the delightful Three Crowns Inn. Sidney Godolphin, a young Cavalier, was killed here during a Civil War skirmish. Elsewhere, it is a pleasure to wander the town's alleys, or to use the town as a base for exploring the western moor. Chagford means 'gorse ford', from the gorse of the moorland, and the ford over the River Teign below the town.

Opposite: Chagford. The poet Sidney Godolphin, shot in the porch of the Three Crowns Inn, is said to haunt it. Another shooting, that of Mary Whyddon, is believed to have given the idea for Lorna Doone's wounding at her wedding

DARTMEET

It is ironic that most visitors to this famous beauty spot do not actually see the point where the East and West Darts Rivers meet, as it lies over 300yd (100m) or so from the road bridge. The East Dart River was probably forded here in prehistoric times. The stepping stones were the next landmark in the evolution of river crossings. Dartmeet also has a clapper bridge, clappers following stepping stones, and a 'modern' arched bridge – the full compliment of crossings. It also has some beautiful river scenery.

DREWSTEIGNTON

Beautifully sited on the moorland edge close to the Teign gorge and Castle Drogo, the village of Drewsteignton forms a square around Holy Trinity Church. The church dates, in part, from the sixteenth century but almost certainly stands on the site of a Saxon building. Julius Drewe of Castle Drogo is buried in the churchyard beneath a granite memorial by Lutyens. Close to the village are not only Castle Drogo, but the Neolithic burial chamber of Spinster's Rock and the Iron Age hillfort of Prestonbury Castle.

Dartmeet is one of Dartmoor's most famous and popular beauty spots. Some visitors, content with the delights of the river crossings – stepping stones, clapper bridge and medieval road bridge – and the East Dart valley do not actually see the point where the East and West Darts meet. This lies to the south of the road bridge

GIDLEIGH

A picturesque – if difficult to find – village with a fine fifteenth-century granite church. Look out for the granite pulpit and lectern. Nearby are the remains of a fourteenth-century castle built by Sir William Prous as a response to the more splendid castle at Okehampton.

HARFORD

A lovely little hamlet comprising little more than a couple of cottages and a beautiful church. Inside the church are a table tomb with a brass effigy in sixteenth-century armour and a painted memorial to John Prideaux, a local man who became Bishop of Worcester. Between Harford and Ivybridge, Lukesland Gardens are 15 acres (6ha) of woodland and landscaped gardens, with pools

and waterfalls. The gardens are famous for their glorious show of azaleas and rhododendrons.

HOLNE

This beautiful little village is known to all walkers of the Two Moors Way as it is often the end-point of the first day for those starting their journey from Ivybridge. The church is fourteenth-century and has a superb carved pulpit. Charles Kingsley, author of *The Water Babies* and *Westward Ho!* was born in the Vicarage in 1819.

HORRABRIDGE

A large, unpretentious village most notable for its medieval bridge, probably the oldest 'modern' bridge on the moor.

ILSINGTON

Close to Haytor, and too often overlooked by those visiting nearby Widecombe-in-the-Moor, this fine village has a lovely church, a lychgate set on granite pillars and St Michael's Cottages, a group including the old Church House (see also Widecombe-in-the-Moor).

IVYBRIDGE

This small town lies outside the National Park and is famous among railway enthusiasts for its viaduct. The original, built by Isambard Kingdom Brunel in wood, was replaced in 1893 by a fine eight-arched granite and brick structure. The town is the starting point for the Two Moors Way, linking Dartmoor with Exmoor.

LYDFORD

I oft have heard of Lydford Law
How in the morn they hang and draw
and sit in judgement after
At first I wondered at it much
But soon I found the matter such
As it deserves no laughter

They have a castle on a hill
I took it for some old windmill
The vanes blown off by the weather.
Than lie therein one night 'tis guessed
'Twere better to be stoned or pressed
Or hanged, ere you come thither.

As mentioned in Chapter 4, Lydford was a Saxon fortress town and mint. Later it was the site of the moor's stannary prison – now called Lydford Castle – a place with a fearsome reputation as the poem printed here maintains.

The church of St Petrock beside the castle is famed for the Watchmaker's Tomb, a table tomb close to the entrance porch with a long and witty inscription.

LUSTLEIGH

The Domesday Book notes Lustleigh's transfer to Ansgar, William the Conqueror's head beekeeper, and that the village was alone in Devon in having a beekeeper.

The village's May Day celebration is one of the most colourful in Devon. The May Queen leads a procession of maypole dancers around the village beneath a canopy of flowers held aloft by four canopy bearers before being crowned with a crown of flowers on a granite boulder in the Town Orchard (across from the church), on which her name is then inscribed.

The village green and church at Manaton

Page100: Holne is one of the most picturesque of Dartmoor villages. The village name means, simply, 'holly' from the trees growing in the sheltered valley. The church is famed for its carved pulpit, painted roof bosses and panelled screen, and for the ancient hollow yew in the churchyard

Page 101: (top) Thatching in Lustleigh; (below) looking up Lustleigh Cleave from Trendlebeare Down

MANATON

Manaton's church needed considerable restoration work after it was damaged in a storm in 1779, testament to the exposed village site. Close to the village are the well-known beauty spot of Becky Falls and its associated woodland; Hound Tor with its medieval village; the curious tor of Bowerman's Nose, and the mysterious Jay's Grave.

MARY TAVY

An old mining village with a nineteenth-century church and a slightly older Methodist chapel. To the north is Wheal Betsy, one of Dartmoor's best preserved mine sites, now in the care of the National Trust. The church in nearby Peter Tavy is older and has an excellent early eighteenth-century carved wall monument to Thomas Peacock.

MEAVY

On the village green stand the old cross and a very old oak tree. The old Church House (see Widecombe-in-the-Moor) is now the Royal Oak Inn. On the wall of the village school is a replica of Drake's Drum, once used to summon children.

MERRIVALE

Merrivale is now little more than an inn, but it was the site of Dartmoor's last granite quarry and one of its most important megalithic complexes. The Four

Winds car park, beside the B3357, is on the site of a former school for quarry-men's children and was once a sheep pound.

MORETONHAMPSTEAD

This lovely little market town should be visited for its fine old buildings, as well as for its position as the gateway to the western moor. The two-storeyed, arcaded almshouses, dating from 1637 are, perhaps, the finest building though the fif-teenth-century church and other buildings near The Square are worth a look. The town was the birthplace in 1806 of George Parker Bidder, famed as 'The Calculating Boy'. He could calculate the cube root of 18-digit numbers in his head in seconds (among other prodigious feats) and became an engineer. He designed and built London's Victoria Docks.

NORTH BOVEY

An extremely picturesque village, including several seventeenth-century thatched houses, gathered around a green beside which is the fine church of St John the

Moretonhampstead is one of the gateways to the moor, a delightful market town set right on the edge of the high plateau. When seen from a distance the town is dominated by its fifteenth-century granite church

Okehampton castle

Baptist. The church has a fifteenth-century carved rood screen. Though much of the original paintwork and gilding has been lost and the screen was vandalised by the Puritans, it is still a marvellous feature.

NORTH BRENTOR/BRENT TOR

North Brentor is a pleasant village with a neat church, dominated by Brent Tor on which stands the famous landmark of St Michael's church. Legend has it that the church was built by a rich merchant returning to Devon who, fearing his ship would be lost in a storm, vowed to build a church if he survived. Another legend claims that the Archangel Michael built the church, but only after a prolonged battle with the Devil. Every night after Michael had worked on the church the Devil would remove the stones. Finally, the exasperated archangel hid to discover the source of his torment. Seeing the Devil, he hurled a granite boulder at him, hitting him on the head. The Devil fled and Michael completed his work.

The church – which tops a cone of basaltic lava rather than Dartmoor granite – dates from the early twelfth century, and seems to have been the work of Robert Giffard, a member of a powerful Norman landowning family in Devon. It is a small, embattled building with a stout tower, and is a landmark for miles around.

OKEHAMPTON

Though lying just outside the National Park, Okehampton is very much a Dartmoor town, occasionally known as the 'Capital of the Northern Moor'. Bypassed by the controversial new A30 dual carriageway, this former bottleneck for holiday makers heading into Cornwall is quieter now, visited by lovers of Devon market towns, walkers heading south towards the military camp and the highest tors, and increasingly by cyclists, who use the National Cycle Network that passes through the town.

The town's strategic importance at the northern fringe of the moor was not lost on Devon's early settlers. The first Norman lord, Baldwin de Brionne, built a castle, later expanded by the Courtenay family who became Earls of Devon. The castle is the largest in Devon and occupies a beautiful site, on a spur of land above the West Okement River. The castle ruins are now in the care of English Heritage. There is a picnic site which makes the most of the picturesque setting, and walks in the bluebell woods that were part of the Earls' deer park and country house when the need for a fortress passed. Legend has it that the ghost of Lady Howard of Fitzford, near Tavistock, visits the site each night to pick a single blade of grass. The story confuses Lady Mary Howard with Lady Frances Howard, who reputedly murdered four husbands and was imprisoned in the Tower of London, but the story is so good that the facts are not allowed to get in the way. Lady Howard is said to change into a black dog which runs beside a coach built of the bones of her dead husbands, driven by a headless coachman and pulled by headless horses. The ensemble follows the old road from Tavistock to the castle, the dog biting off one blade of grass before the party heads back to Fitzford.

The Courtenay castle encouraged the development of the market town below it, and Okehampton is still worth an exploration. Be sure to visit the Museum of Dartmoor Life in West Street with its displays on the history of Man on the moor.

POSTBRIDGE

Postbridge has one of Dartmoor's most famous and picturesque clapper bridges. It is also one of the largest, with a span of 42ft (13m), and has the tallest pillars of any Dartmoor clapper, the East Dart River being prone to severe flooding. The road heading south from the village is said to be haunted by a pair of hairy hands which grab steering wheels and handlebars in an effort to force drivers off the road.

PRINCETOWN

As noted in Chapter 4, Princetown was built by Thomas Tyrwhitt and named for the Prince of Wales. After building the prison, Tyrwhitt built a railway, in part to service his quarries but also to bring lime to sweeten the moorland soil, hoping the town would be the centre of a rich farming area. The railway was completed in 1827 and much of it became part of GWR, but it was never profitable and finally closed in 1956.

The town church is said to be the only one in England to have been built by prisoners, with French and American PoWs responsible. after the prison had been completed. Princetown is now home to the excellent National Park's Authority High Moorland Visitor Centre.

SAMPFORD SPINEY

A secluded hamlet between Pew Tor and the Walkham valley. The old manor house, now a farm, dates from the seventeenth century.

SHAUGH PRIOR

A linear village close to the beautiful Plym Valley, with the Dewerstone outcrop to the north-west, and the china clay works of Lee Moor to the east and north-east.

Prisoners' graves at Princetown

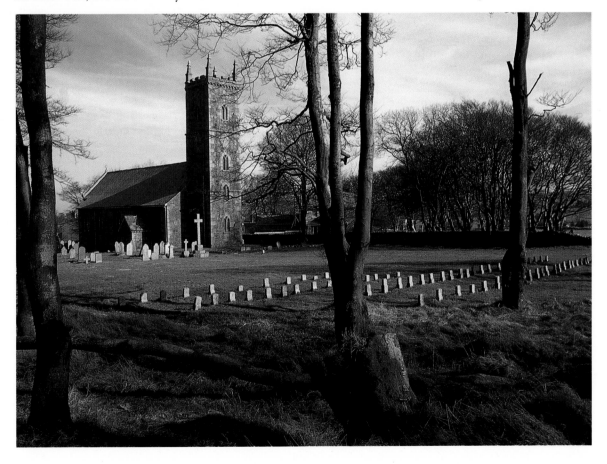

Above: Sheepstor

Opposite: (top) Finch Foundry, Sticklepath; (below) Yarnapitts, Throwleigh

The village has terraced cottages built for china clay workers during the early years of the industry. The medieval font cover in the church is said to have been discovered in a local cattle shed. There is a Church House (see Widecombe-in-the-Moor) in the churchyard.

SHEEPSTOR

Be sure to see the strange carving above the church's front porch. It dates from the seventeenth century and shows a skull, with bones in its mouth and ears of corn sprouting from its eye sockets, above an hourglass.

In the churchyard are the graves of three English-born Rajahs of Sarawak. The first, James Brooke, went to Sarawak as an official to thank the Rajah for his kindness to a group of shipwrecked British sailors. Finding the country over-run by pirates, he restored peace and was made Rajah by the grateful locals. He was succeeded to the title by two other members of the Brooke family.

SOUTH BRENT

As at Lydford and nearby Harford, the church is dedicated to St Petroc, the early Celtic saint. St Petroc's is an early Norman foundation, though much restored, sitting picturesquely above the River Avon. The road which heads northwards beside the river reaches a car park close to Hunter's Stone (so called because it is inscribed with the names of hunting friends), from where walkers can follow the

Zeal Tramway to Petre's Cross and Huntingdon Warren, or the private road to the Avon Dam Reservoir.

SOUTH ZEAL

South Zeal is a medieval 'new town' (if that is not a contradiction), created as a market town by Norman lord Robert de Tony in the thirteenth century. It is famous as the home of the Oxenham family – remembered in the name of the village inn – the deaths of whose members were foretold by a white dove fluttering above their heads. Most famously, the bird hovered above Margaret Oxenham on the eve of her wedding. As she was in full health the omen was ignored, but she was stabbed to death in the church by a jealous lover who then killed himself.

STICKLEPATH

This neat little village is famous among geologists for the Sticklepath Fault, which has displaced a section of the north-eastern moor. Well worth visiting is the National Trust's Finch Foundry, a restored early nineteenth-century forge powered by three waterwheels.

TAVISTOCK

Though Tavistock lies just outside the National Park, few visitors will miss an exploration of this charming market town, another of

Dartmoor's former stannary towns. Tavistock grew up around a Benedictine abbey founded in the late tenth century, one of the richest on the peninsula when it was dissolved by Henry VIII. The ruins can be seen near Bedford Square. The nearby church of St Eustace dates from the early fourteenth century and is built in fine Perpendicular style. The Pannier Market, first held in 1105, takes place on Fridays in a building behind the Town Hall.

THROWLEIGH

A secluded village with a restored granite church beside which is an early sixteenth-century church house. At nearby Higher Shilstone there is a fine sixteenth-century longhouse, the best on Dartmoor from that period.

Uncle Tom Cobley and all ...

TWO BRIDGES

The bridges cross the Cowsic and West Dart Rivers close to their confluence. The inn here is popular with walkers, and magical Wistman's Wood lies just to the north, while Crockern Tor, site of the Stannary Parliament, is to the north-east.

WALKHAMPTON

The church stands away from the rest of the village in one of the most dramatic settings on the moor. The large granite tower adds to the drama of the location. Close to the church stands the Church House which has been converted into private dwellings. The village school is Victorian, replacing a very early foundation of 1719.

WIDECOMBE-IN-THE-MOOR

There is a lot more to Widecombe-in-the-Moor than Uncle Tom Cobley and all. The parish church, sometimes called the Cathedral of the Moor because of its tall, magnificent tower, is said to have been built, in part, with money donated by local tin miners.

Next to the church is Church House. Church houses, often called church ale-houses, were built as church halls and village meeting rooms. They would also be used as brew houses, the beer being sold with food, to the congregation. This was particularly welcomed by folk who had travelled from outlying farms. The profits from the sales helped towards the upkeep of the church. The Church House here, which dates to 1537, is one of few that remain and is now in the care of the National Trust, though it remains the village hall. The Sexton's Cottage beside the Church House is now an Information Centre. Opposite the church house is the village green, to the west of which is the Old Inn which dates from the fourteenth century.

The Fair which the old song has made famous is still held annually in September.

YELVERTON

A large village on the edge of the National Park. To the west, just outside the National Park, is Buckland Abbey, once the home of Sir Francis Drake, now in the care of the National Trust. The abbey has a collection of Drake memorabilia (including the famous Drake's Drum), and exhibitions on the Spanish Armada and the abbey's own history. In Yelverton itself, the Paperweight Centre is a private collection of several hundred paperweights, including many unusual examples.

Information

USEFUL ADDRESSES

Dartmoor National Park Authority
Parke, Haytor Road
Bovey Tracey
Devon TQ13 9JQ
Tel: 01626 832093
www.dartmoor-npa.gov.uk

National Park Information Centres

Lower Car Park on the main road
near Haytor
Tel: 01364 661520

Riverside Car Park at Newbridge
Tel: 01364 631303

Car Park at Postbridge
Tel: 01822 880272

High Moorland Visitor Centre
Tavistock Road, Princetown
Tel: 01822 890414

Local Information Points:
Ashburton Information Centre,
Tel: 01364 653426
Moretonhampstead Information
Centre, Tel: 01647 440043

West Country Tourist Board
Trinity Court
60 St David's Hill
Exeter
Devon EX4 4SY
Tel: 01392 425426

Devon Tourism
Devon County Council
County Hall
Exeter
Devon EX2 4QQ
Tel: 01392 382284

Dartmoor Tourist Association
The Duchy Building
Tavistock Road
Princetown
Devon PL20 6QF
Tel: 01822 890567

Facilities for Disabled Visitors

Countryside Access Group for
Dartmoor
Parke
Haytor Road
Bovey Tracey
Devon TQ13 9JQ
Tel: 01626 832093

or contact individual organisations:

Riding for the Disabled
Association
Tel: 01752 894348

Devon County Association
for the Blind
Tel: 01392 876666

Other Bodies

Devon Wildlife Trust
35 St David's Hill
Exeter
EX4 4DA
Tel: 01392 279244

English Heritage
Customer Services
PO Box 9019
London
W1A 0JA
Tel: 0171 973 3434

Forestry Commission
(Forestry Enterprise)
Bullers Hill
Kennford
Exeter
Devon EX6 7XR
Tel: 01392 832262

The National Trust
Devon Regional Office
Killerton House
Broadclyst
Exeter
Devon EX5 3LF
Tel: 01392 881691

South-West Water
Fisheries and Recreation Office
Peninsula House
Rydon Lane
Exeter
Devon EX2 7HR
Tel: 01837 871565

Youth Hostels Association
11b York Road
Salisbury
Wiltshire SP2 7AP
Tel: 01271 324420
(There are Youth Hostels at
Okehampton, Steps Bridge and
Bellever)

*For information on public transport on
Dartmoor, contact:*

Devon Bus Enquiry Lines:
Tel: 01392 382800

*For information on the Dartmoor
military ranges, contact the answering
services on:*

Tel: 01837 52939 (Okehampton)

Local Attractions

Ashburton Town Museum
West Street
Ashburton
Tel: 01364 652648

Becky Falls
Manaton
Tel: 01647 221259

Buckfast Abbey
Buckfast
Tel: 01364 642519

Buckfast Butterflies and Otter
Sanctuary
Buckfastleigh
Tel: 01364 642916

Buckland Abbey (National Trust)
Yelverton
Tel: 01822 853607

Castle Drogo (National Trust)
Drewsteignton
Tel: 01647 433306

Devon Guild of Craftsmen
Riverside Mill
Bovey Tracey
Tel: 01626 832223

Finch Foundry (National Trust)
Sticklepath
Tel: 01837 840046

House of Marbles and Teign Valley
Glass
The Old Pottery, Pottery Road
Bovey Tracey
Tel: 01626 835358

Lukesland Gardens
Harford
Tel: 01752 893390

Lydford Gorge (National Trust)
Lydford
Tel: 01822 820441/820320

Miniature Pony Centre
North Bovey
Tel: 01647 432400

Museum of Dartmoor Life
3 West Street
Okehampton
Tel: 01837 52295

Okehampton Castle (English
Heritage)
Tel: 01837 52844

River Dart Country Park
Holne Park
Ashburton
Tel: 01364 652511

Yelverton Paperweight Centre
Leg o' Mutton
Yelverton
Tel: 01822 854250

MAPS

The use of the excellent
appropriate Ordnance Survey
maps is highly recommended for
any detailed exploration of the
National Park, especially if you
are leaving the car behind and
venturing out into the
countryside.

Outdoor Leisure Map (1:25,000)
No 28 Dartmoor
Landrangers (1:50,000) No 191
Okehampton & North Dartmoor;
No 202 Torbay & South
Dartmoor, Totnes & Salcombe

FURTHER READING

Cherry, Bridget, and Pevsner,
    Nikolaus. *The Buildings of
    England*, Devon (Penguin, 1989)
Crossing, William. *Crossing's Guide
    to Dartmoor* (First published
    1909, reprinted Peninsula Press,
    1993)
Greeves, Tom. *The Archaeology of
    Dartmoor from the Air* (Devon
    Books/Dartmoor National Park,
    1985)
Harris, Helen. *Industrial
    Archaeology of Dartmoor* (David &
    Charles, 1968)
Hemery, Eric. *Walking the
    Dartmoor Waterways* (David &
    Charles, 1986)
Hoskins, Prof W.G. ed. *Dartmoor
    National Park* (HMSO, 1957)
Prince, Elizabeth, and Head, John.
    Dartmoor Seasons (Devon
    Books/Dartmoor National Park,
    1987)
Sale, Richard. *Collins Ramblers'
    Guide: Dartmoor* (Harper
    Collins, 2000)
Weir, John, ed. *Dartmoor National
    Park* (Webb & Bower/Michael
    Joseph, 1987)
Worth, R. Hansford. *Worth's
    Dartmoor* (First published, 1953,
    reprinted Peninsula Press, 1994)

Index

Page numbers in *italics* indicate illustrations